Tonquish Tales

Best Wishes

Helen Frances Gilbert

Pictured on the cover is a watercolor by an unknown, but probably Detroit, artist. The work is dated 1794. It is reproduced here by courtesy of the Burton Historical Collection of the Detroit Public Library. It was a gift to them by Lady Nancy Astor, who discovered it in Plymouth, England.

Fort Lernoult, or, as it was commonly called, Fort Detroit, was solidly constructed in anticipation of a raid by Colonel George Rogers Clark and his Kentuckians. It was named in honor of Captain Richard B. Lernoult, the military officer in charge of its construction.

Many long years have gone by since Antoine Cadillac and his Frenchmen had built Fort Ponchartrain and the old war house was rather shaky. It had survived fires and floods, invasions by the Fox Indians and others, and the wear and tear of constant traffic. It was doubtful if it could have withstood the fire power of the "Long Knives," as the Indians called the Kentuckians.

Note the half bastions and the earthen ramparts. Fire could be directed from almost any angle. There was a ditch in front of the rampart, and a palisade in the center section. Beyond this was a low earthen barricade called a glacis, and beyond that was an abatis of felled wood with a strong barricade of sharp wooden spikes. Lernoult's Fort was ready for anything, and Detroit was well protected.

Fort Lernoult was built in back of the little town in an area about where the Detroit Bank & Trust (Comerica) building stands today.

2

Tonquish Tales

A story of early d'Etroit, pioneers and
Michigan Indians.

by

Helen Frances Gilbert

A Publication of the
Pilgrim Heritage Press
Plymouth, Michigan
P. O. Box 473
48170

ISBN 0-9622346-0-5

To order additional copies of
Tonquish Tales write:

Ms. Helen Gilbert
C/o Plymouth Heritage Books
P.O. Box 6315
Plymouth, MI.
48170

Printed by Braun Brumfield, Inc.

4

This book was written with
happy thoughts and wonderful memories
of my dear parents

Letitia Smith Gilbert

whose unfailing devotion to her family,
to her friends, and to her ideals
helped to shape the life of her daughter,
And to my dear father

Benjamin Ray Gilbert

an honorable, kind, and gentle man
whose advice and wisdom were esteemed
by all who truly knew him.
> To them
> this book
> is most affectionately
> Dedicated

Contents

Dear Reader,

This copy of
Tonquish Tales is
number_____

This edition is limited

to 1,000 copies.

Good wishes and
happy reading

_____

Helen Gilbert

Preface

Tonquish Tales first appeared in the Plymouth Observer-Eccentric, a newspaper distributed in western Wayne County, Michigan, in 1982. Sometimes more than the usual fortnight elapsed between columns, and so it was necessary to begin each story with the highlights of the preceding one. While this lent clarity to the pertinent facts for the first time reader, to someone familiar with the tale it may have seemed repetitious. I have tried to remove this redundancy.

President John F. Kennedy wrote in his introduction to William Brandon's excellent "Book of Indians" (in the American Heritage series): "For a subject worked and reworked so often in novels, motion pictures, and television, American Indians remain probably the least understood and most misunderstood Americans of us all. American Indians defy any single description. They were and are far too individualistic. They shared no common language and few common customs. But collectively their history is our history and should be part of our shared and remembered heritage."

Any fair assessment of stories about the American Indian must take into account that we are exploring the history of a people who left us no written language. Their cultural remnants and sign language sometimes lead to a variety of interpretations. The Indian has often been misrepresented and misunderstood because of ignorance of his true condition and beliefs. And the plight of these native Americans has been made worse by exploitation, political chicanery, and selfish greed. A consistently more humane and reasonably truthful approach to the Indian is long overdue.

Few writers have achieved an unbiased, unprejudiced approach to this subject. Some of the best writers in this field are listed in the bibliography at the end of this book.

Napoleon Bonaparte once said, "What is history, but a fable agreed upon?" Hendrik VanLoon in "The Story of Mankind" said, "The history of the world is the record of a man in quest of his daily bread and butter." Both of these elements—fables and food—are a part of Tonquish Tales. We leave you, gentle reader, to distinguish between the two.

Acknowledgments

The author wishes to express her thanks to many individuals who have been consistently helpful in the preparation of this book. On my long list of people who will be gratefully remembered are many reference librarians at the Library of Congress, at the University of Michigan, at the Burton Historical Collections of the Detroit Public Library, the Dearborn Public Library, the Public Library of Ann Arbor, the Columbus Library of the Ohio Historical Society, Chicago's Newberry Library, the Michigan State Library in Lansing, the Michigan State University Library in East Lansing, and Western Michigan University Library and the City Library of Kalamazoo as well as our local facility, the Dunning-Hough Library here in Plymouth. Unfailingly kind, cooperative, and patient these helpful librarians will long be remembered.

The great libraries of the University of Michigan including the William L. Clements Library, the Bentley Historical Collections, The Law Library, and the Library of the Graduate School all afford excellent resources for the historical researcher. (A list of references consulted in the preparation of this book may be found at the end of the last chapter.)

Acknowledgments would be incomplete without a special "thank-you" to several friends who read the manuscript and offered helpful advice including Father Robert Shank of St. John's Episcopal Church, Plymouth, Dr. Mary Margaret Fritz, Mr. Warren Gilbert, and Dr. Donald Gilbert.

Others who were helpful in different ways include: Mrs. Jewett Pokagon, whose husband was a grandson of Chief Simon Pokagon. Informative and knowledgeable, her memories of the past were appreciated.

Michele Gauthier granted permission to use her prize-winning portrait, Winter Ojibway. This excellent portrait won a Purchase Award in the Michigan Historical Museums Show "Images of Michigan's Heritage." It now hangs in the Mason County Courthouse.

The Detroit Institute of Arts granted permission to use a notable painting by Albert Bierstadt. The Burton Collection loaned the wonderful picture of "Detroit in 1794." The Northern Indiana Historical Society gave us rights to the Van Sanden portrait of Leopold Pokagon. The Grand Rapids Library Heritage Room loaned the portrait of Luther Livingston.

Most of all, I would thank the public who have purchased more than a thousand copies of this little book in about a year. This is the long promised second edition. I trust that there are a thousand more readers out there who will enjoy my version of Michigan in the days of the Indian and Cadillac's d'Etroit.

> Happy Reading to you.
> Helen Gilbert

Tonquish Tales

A story of pioneers and Indians
in the early days of southern Michigan

"The Winter Ojibway" by Michele Gauthier.

The artist has carefully researched the accouterments that are penned in this picture. They are authentic. Ishikawa, judge of "Images of Michigan's Heritage" at the Michigan Historical Museum, said it is "masterfully done" showing "no condescension." I think it is even more than that. It has a kind of courageous, spiritual quality that transcends betrayal, deprivation, and death. Chief Tonquish was of that race and spirit.

1. Chief Tonquish and His Family Wage Fight for Survival

After the glacial waters receded—many milleniums ago—huge layers of ice covered the Plymouth-Canton area and all of Michigan.

Eventually the earth began to dry out and the beautiful lakes and rivers we know today emerged from the deluge.

About 10,000 years ago (geologists' estimates vary widely but it was just yesterday in the continuum of time-space), the Niagara gorge was shaped and the Great Lakes of Michigan were defined.

Yesterday the forests grew, the flowers blossomed in the returning sun, and the song of the meadow lark was heard upon the good earth. Just yesterday the good earth opened her arms to a strange, migratory people we call the Indians.

Many moons ago, long before Chief Tonquish staked his claim to the Plymouth-Canton area, the nights were brightened by the campfires of his ancestors.

At a place the French called d'Etroit the fires of Tonquish's people rimmed both sides of the river as far as Lake St. Clair and beyond.

Chief Tonquish made his mark on treaties as a Chippewa but it is believed that his surviving wife was a Potowatomi and associated with the Pokagon clan. We do know that Tonquish was an Algonquin, and whether Chippewa or Potowatomi, he belonged to an important branch of the great Algonquin nation. This branch was the Ojibwa of Canada. At one time the Algonquin controlled the largest area ever occupied by the North American Indian.

Their territory extended from the Rocky Mountains east to Labrador, and from the uppermost part of Manitoba to the borders of North Carolina. They were in the Detroit area a century or two before the French priests arrived in the 1660s.

In fact, when the long boats of the Vikings pushed onto the rocky shore of Maine—long before Columbus and 1492—they found Algonquin living where they always had lived along the Atlantic coast.

About 600-years ago, sometime in the 1300s (the exact date is unknown), the Ojibwa of the Algonquin began a great westward movement. They were pressured by an expanding population, internal dissensions, crop failures and the fierce hostility of the Iroquois.

First, they moved to the Montreal area where some remain to this day; others came to Detroit. Some went to Sault Ste. Marie and others to Wisconsin. When the Tonquish group (the Potowatomi) reached Michilimackinac, they joined with two other groups—the Chippewas and the Ottawas—in a federation for mutual protection. They called this consortium "The Three Fires," and the Chippewa were called "The Elder Brothers." Back in the very early ages they probably came from one tribe. All three could understand each other, and spoke in Algonquian dialect which had some variations among the three but was their common trade language.

Tonquish's Potowatomis were dependent upon hunting, fishing, trapping and some agriculture for their survival.

The other alternative was stealing, and in the latter days of the tribe in Wayne County they took full advantage of that option.

Their old style was to leave their oval, dome-shaped, skin-thatched shelter early in the morning and begin the hunt for the day's food.

The home of Chief Tonquish was laid on two bent poles and easily could be transported. When the winter winds began, the whole clan with Tonquish (or Toga as he commonly was called) on the lead pony, migrated to new territory for the winter hunt. Usually they went southward, sometimes as far as the Ohio River or southern Indiana.

Today the Potowatomis have enclaves on Walpole Island and in Calhoun County, in Dowagiac and St. Joseph. The general exodus to the west that the government planned for them in the 1830s was not entirely successful. Many refused to go and some drifted back to their old stamping grounds in Michigan.

Today they lend their colorful charm to Michigan's multi-hued coat of many races. Independent and willful as always, they have not been easily assimilated into the main stream of the white-man's culture.

Chief Tonquish (or Toga) was a nephew of the supreme chief of the Potowatomi—a remarkably intelligent Indian named Topenebee.

Topenebee presided at the signing of the famous treaty of Greenville, Aug 3, 1795. This provided the first cession of Indian lands in Michigan to the white man.

The year 1796 saw the evacuation of the British from their remaining posts in Michigan. After many years of warfare between the frontiersmen and the Indians, many small battles, too detailed to relate here, ended for a time. But not for long. In 1812 the British came back and the terrible war of that year wreaked havoc upon the colonists in the Plymouth-Canton area along the Rouge River.

Among the horrors of the War of 1812 was the British capture of the city of Washington and the wanton burning of some of our public buildings including the total destruction of many priceless national records.

Although we had won some brilliant victories on the water, particularly that of Commodore Perry at Lake Erie, we suffered dismal losses on land. In time we fumbled our way to a tired victory. The peace Treaty of Ghent on the day before Christmas 1814 said nothing about any of the greivances which we had complained of when the war began.

One of the worst horrors of that time was the massacre at Fort Dearborn. More than 500 Potowatomi came down their old trails along the Huron, the Rouge, and the Tonquish to join in a massacre of the garrison at Fort Dearborn, now a part of Chicago.

Chief Tonquish was in the vanguard of that slaughter. Only Topenebee, a Tonquish relative, among the Potowatomi chiefs advised against the brutal action at Dearborn and Topenebee tried to shelter the few survivors.

Memories of the Dearborn massacre and other wartime events help to explain the contempt with which Tonquish was held by many of the settlers. And the memory of that slaughter must have been with Captain McComb that day in October 1819 when he stood on the Tonquish Plains and aimed straight at Toga's heart.

2. Chief Tonquish Slain by Militia

Among the poor settlers along the Rouge River was one Alanson Thomas. Thomas had hand-crafted a rude cabin on his newly-cleared lands on the north side of the river near the fort in Dearborn.

Alanson was proud of his little homestead and he was busy improving its limited amenities. One rainy day, while working on some shelves for his wife's convenience, Thomas was interrupted by a bold Indian dressed in the fancy garb of a chief. Rudely pushing his way into the cabin, the Indian demanded "fire water."

Thomas recognized Toga and ordered him out. He probably said, "Get the hell out of here," or stronger words to that effect. Whatever he said enraged Toga and he sprang at Thomas as if to kill him. The plucky Welshman aimed one mighty blow at Toga's chin and the chief was knocked senseless.

A band of Indians witnessed his plight but they did not make a move. They stood motionless. Only one stepped forward to rescue the old chief. It was his only son, the young Toga. As he assisted his father he threatened Thomas with, "Bimby you be dead. Bimby, Thomas dead." Although the Thomases lived in fear for a decade, Toga and his clan never bothered them again.

One day in the fall of 1819 Tonquish and his son were out foraging for food—"borrowing" here and there as was their custom. In their entourage that day were three squaws, many children and a posse of young braves spoiling for trouble.

Trouble came on the wind. It came with the aroma of Mrs. Sargent's freshly-baked bread. Floating over the tranquil waters of the Rouge it inspired the whole clan to dreams of a feast. Quickly beaching their canoes near the Sargent's they rushed into the cabin, appropriated all the bread and promptly departed.

Mr. Sargent happened to return home just at the moment of their leave-taking and he bravely plunged into the stream, retrieving some of the loaves. Just as he crossed the threshold of his little home Toga's son shot him dead.

This incident thoroughly aroused the settlers in our area. They hastily organized themselves into a fighting posse and pursued the fleeing culprits as closely as they could. A few of the settlers made a hasty journey into Detroit to arouse the militia.

Toga and his Indians fled up the Rouge to its confluence with the west branch which they followed up the north side.

The irate settlers finally caught up with them near where the old Potowatomi trail crossed the town line between Nankin and Livonia. This is located a little west of the mill pond that used to be called Nankin Mills.

At that point Tonquish and his braves passed out of sight. It was magical—utterly amazing! The settlers could not believe it. They were there and then suddenly they were gone. They were hiding in secret places known only to Toga.

Suddenly the settlers were startled by a savage shout and the Indians arose from their ambush and fired into them. No one was seriously hurt.

The settlers immediately advanced upon the Indians before they could reload their old guns and the Indians, outnumbered and outgunned, quickly were captured. Only two got away—Chief Tonquish and his son escaped. Fleet as deer, amazingly agile! But their freedom was only temporary. Soon McComb and the militia from Fort Detroit came to the settler's rescue.

McComb brought fresh horses, better guns, and plenty of ammunition. And the hunt began. After hours of zig-zag running McComb caught up with old Toga and his son. Although frightened the old chief was determined to fight to the bitter end.

Tonquish sprang out of his concealment in a hollow tree almost in front of McComb who ordered him to halt. The chief paused, pretended to obey, but his born-free son kept on running. McComb, a crack shot, took dead aim at the young man's fleeing back. Seeing this the chief yelled, "McComb. Wait! Wait! Me bring him back. He no go. Me stop him!"

I suppose it is to the captain's credit that he paused, and all the settlers paused too. It was as though the drama had some mystical significance. They were tired, winded; they had run for miles. But everyone waited. Everyone! It was at this very moment that time stood still. Perhaps Tonquish knew the old ways were leaving. What followed would change this place forever. The people seemed to know this. They watched and they waited.

Then old Chief Tonquish in a stern and commanding voice, and in the Indian language (this is roughly translated Potowatomi) yelled, "Run like hell, son. Run with the wind, son. He kill you. Go to Topenebee. Topenebee. Run. Hell. Run."

When young Toga had reached some distance, a distance his father judged to be beyond the range of Macomb's gun, then and only then, Tonquish suddenly feigned anger and rage. He shouted, "McComb, damn him! He no come back. McComb. Shoot him."

McComb shot that sure shot and young Toga fell dead.

Seeing his son destroyed, Tonquish drew a knife which he had concealed in his shirt and sprang at McComb. Sgt. James Bucklin, the major's aide, rushed to his side and, using his own gun, was able to protect the Captain from Toga's blows. Then Tonquish tried to run but he didn't get very far.

The old records say he was shot in the back while trying to escape. When he finally fell, running some distance even after he had been mortally shot, he gave fierce expression to his rage and grief. Ripping the soil with his knife he uttered an angry, disconsolate growl reminiscent of a dying bear. That night he finally died.

The next day the Potowatomi came to the place to bury the chief and his son. Their ritual ceremony accorded him the great respect reserved for an important chief. When they had finished they built a protective fence around the two graves. There they remained undisturbed until about 1837 when a gang of mischievous boys opened the graves, took what was left of the chief's gun and all the small trinkets Indians leave with their dead to assure their passage into a better world.

This event took place in Section 4 of the township of Nankin about one mile west of land which for many years was known as the Dimmick farm. It would be a relatively easy task to pinpoint the spot on any good old atlas after a survey of the probate records. I have not done so because I think it is probably paved over by the latest development in our own concrete jungle.

The Potowatomi, according to old legends, worshipped at a secret shrine near Plymouth.

All their feast days were celebrated here. And their altar, a masterpiece in carved stone, is supposed to be extant somewhere in our area.

My research has led me to believe that that altar may be in one of three places. (I base this upon rather sketchy evidence). Some 60 years ago I remember being in Sunday School at the First Presbyterian Church when somebody told the story of how workmen had come upon people sitting up in their graves in a nearby cemetery. I have since learned that this is a custom of some Potowatomi.

With this in mind I recently asked Rev. Philip Rodgers McGee of the First United Presbyterian Church of Plymouth what he knew about Indians being buried in the old graveyard. He told me that when they dug the basement for the chapel they came upon many Indian relics. Could it be that the old graveyard near the church once was sacred ground to the Potowatomi? Does it hold their altar?

Another possibility is the old cemetery on North Territorial near Ridgewood. I have heard that many Indians are buried in that area. Why don't we explore this and rescue that graveyard from the oblivion that is rapidly overtaking it?

A third guess locates the altar on a hill by the mysterious and beautiful little lake near what used to be the fifth hole at Fox Hills Country Club. What is your guess?

We should call the walkway to Tonquish Manor, Toga's Lane. Fifty years ago I found a penny there dated 1803! The path probably has many tales to tell.

3. Telonga Named New Chief of Tonquish Indian Clan

After almost a lifetime—more than 60 years—ensconced near the banks of the sometimes turbulent Tonquish, it is not unnatural for me to make further inquiry into the events that have marked its colorful past.

Among those events there is one that rings a holiday bell. It includes a celebration, a fellowship of feasting and music, and group worship at the sacred altar under the pines of Plymouth mound.

And, sad to relate, in the end there is a kind of sacramental crucifixion for a young brave who had violated the clan's moral code.

This story reveals the significance of certain strongly-held moral values in the so-called "savage" mind.

Once again the winds of winter herald the time when the whole clan, en masse, begins its migration southward.

It is late in November 1819. The clan has buried Chief Tonquish (Toga) and his son with all due honor.

Now the winter hunt in search of fresh game must begin. But the structure of their organization also demands that they pause, settle their differences, and name a new chief.

Fierce arguments have arisen among them. Tonquish, their peacemaker and guide, who had always controlled them with a kind of benevolent dictatorship, is not there to soothe their troubled spirits. His leadership is greatly missed. Their survival as a group now is at stake.

But it must be remembered that the Potowatomi have a long history of survival in difficult times. Outgunned (but not always outfought) by an army of "palefaces" in hot pursuit, the Plymouth Potowatomi always seem to survive. They cling to their old lands and their old ways with an integrity and belief that command our admiration.

Custom decreed that their old men—"the wise ones," the elders of the tribe—should name Toga's successor. They alone had that power.

But in the Plymouth clan there was an ambitious, foolhardy group of young braves determined to have their way. They called Toga's death an unnecessary murder, and they mourned his young son as a dear friend, a beloved hunting companion, and titular head of their generation of young, hunting braves. They never forgave Captain McComb and the settlers for Toga's death.

As the days of decision wore on it became increasingly difficult for the Plymouth elders to restrain these hotheaded youngsters. And the rebellious generation was joined by a few disgruntled old braves who had their own axes to grind and so encouraged the mischief. Once again there was open talk of another massacre like the one at Fort Dearborn.

The old diaries indicate that the white settlers along the Rouge were fully aware of the dissension among the local Potowatomi, and they were as anxious as the Indian elders that a new chief be found—and soon!

Finally, after many confrontations and pow wows, endless

smoke, talk, talk, talk far into the unforgiving, relentless night, it became apparent to the elders that there was no end to the argument.

So they sent two fleet-footed messengers to their supreme chief, Topenebee, at his place near Silver Creek in Cass County.

Chief Topenebee was old and ill, although his mind was as shrewd and incisive as ever—a very superior mind.

The prospect of the long journey to the high altar in Plymouth did not please him. He was a proud Indian. After all, he had been one of the Potowatomi chiefs who had signed the Treaty of Greenville on Aug. 3, 1795. This treaty provided for the first cession of Indian lands in Michigan to the Americans.

Topenebee, almost alone among the great chiefs of the Potowatomi, had refused to participate in the massacre of the American garrison at Fort Dearborn at the outbreak of the War of 1812.

Topenebee alone sheltered and protected the few survivors at some risk to himself and to his own braves.

Don't misunderstand this. It is not interpreted as anything more than shrewd, diplomatic jockeying for some advantage. Topenebee was motivated by political considerations and the need to protect his people against the relentless, incoming tide of pale faces.

Christianity, as we know it today, was not meaningful to the Potowatomi of that time and place, but the advance of the white man surely was. Topenebee was as much of a savage in his life, his beliefs, and in his actions as any other full-blooded Indian. Only his thoughts were somewhat different. His remarkable mind placed him above the usual Indian passion and prejudice.

Independent and stubborn, he never sold his people short. And that cannot be said of all the Potowatomi chiefs. More than any other chief since the great Pontiac, Topenebee listened to his own thoughts and marched to his own drummer.

So the elders of Plymouth knew what they were doing when they sought his aid to settle their dispute.

From the evidence I have examined it appears that Topenebee thought that going to Plymouth to settle some piddling argument as to who would be minor chief along the little valley of the Rouge was, after all, beneath his dignity.

He is reported to have said, "Let them settle their own fights or live with it," or words to that effect. But he was pressured to change his mind, and after considerable thought over night, he came back in the morning with a counter offer.

He had come to a decision. He sent to Plymouth his right-hand bower, his nephew and adopted son, and the man closest to his heart, Leopold Pokagon. And with Pokagon he also sent an aide and a candidate for leadership of the Tonquish Indians—an ambitious, handsome, young brave, Telonga.

Upon several occasions in the past Telonga had challenged the authority of Topenebee himself. All three of these Indian notables were blood relatives of the late Chief Tonquish.

Perhaps Topenebee saw in Telonga someone for whom the young Plymouth rebels would have some empathy. He probably envisioned solving his own problems and the near rebellion on Tonquish Plains with one swift, diplomatic move. These are logical conjectures from the known facts. Let us see what happened.

Telonga or Tongah (whose Indian name is not easily translated but this is a close approximation) walked confidently with Pokagon under the pines of Plymouth and faced a multitude of angry dissidents.

Exactly what was said is lost in the shroud of buried history. But Telonga, only thirty summers young, had a special kind of magic, a kind of charisma and confidence which impressed the young rebels and, for the first time, the muttering ceased.

They listened quietly as Pokogan spoke of the will of Topenebee, and once again the wisdom and the will of Topenebee prevailed.

So it came to pass that Telonga became chief of the Potowatomi of Tonquish Plains and the valley of the Rouge.

Next time we meet I will take you to the ceremony under the pines on the sacred mound at Plymouth, and I will tell you of the happiness and of the sorrow Telonga brought to Toga's tribe.

4. Ceremony for Indian Royalty Held on Mound at Plymouth

When the sun tolled the day and the dawn broke on Tonquish Plain, the elders said it was a good omen for their new chief.

Now it is early December 1819 and long past the time when the winter hunt should begin.

But today Toga's clan, with some friendly Indians from neighboring clans, a number of cross-cousins from Cass County and Walpole Island, and a few invited white guests from the trading post will celebrate the installation of Telonga, their new chief.

It is early dawn and three young Tonquish braves are wrestling with a huge stone near the base of Plymouth Mound.

The braves are dressed in colorful, ceremonial garb including elaborate head feathers, silver earrings, leggings tinkling with a hundred tin bells. On their feet are jeweled moccasins ornamented with beads, tufts of deer's hair, and porcupine quills.

The rock seems to be in two pieces. One is a fire pot. The larger piece, the pot's base, is a solid rock of hammered stone, Intricately carved around its perimeter is a winding snake—symbol of life and power. In the background is a large sun and a number of stars. Scattered among the stars are symbols of fertility and faith.

The favorite symbol of the Potowatomi is the decorated fire pot itself. It will hold what they believe to be is the immortal fire of the Gods. It has been said that the word Potowatomi means "keepers of the fire," Nowhere in their nation, so it was believed, does the fire ever die out. This is their sacred altar, shrouded in the mystery of Plymouth Mound.

At nearby Tonquish Creek the braves find their Indian pony. They tie him with a makeshift halter and bring him to the stone. With his help they are able to load it on a flatbed sledge which the pony drags to the top of the Mound.

While the young braves are struggling with this project, the squaws are cooking the meat which the hunting braves had killed. All week long the older hunters have searched for game. They brought fresh salmon from the river near Ft. Detroit, and their arrows found plenty of venison and buffalo meat, many squirrels and other small game. The old hunters now are resting while the squaws prepare the feast.

The women have worked half the night at the task.

They have filled three large brass kettles and several iron ones with their good cooking. But, like housewives everywhere, they are worrying if they have enough.

Their menu consists of boiled jerky, fish, baked salmon, stewed, spiced squirrel, roasted venison, and roast buffalo meat. In one large pot they have green corn, some of it cut from the cob, mixed with beans into a kind of succotash. And there are dozens of baked squashes and fresh roasted pumpkins.

The squaws are bustling about in their party finery, disregarding the possibility of damage or stain. Their colorful calico shirts extend about six inches below the waist and are fastened at the bosom with silver brooches. They are wrapped in a full skirt held by an ornamented girdle. Their leggings are Indian stockings sewed to fit the leg perfectly, and their moccasins are elaborately ornamented with beaded rybands and porcupine quills.

Each squaw's basic costume is about the same—the difference is in the ornamentation. All the young, and the middle-aged women too, are passionately fond of ornaments. Their silver brooches are status symbols, and among the leading elder's wives were many silver bracelets and elaborate earrings. All wore fancy borders on the bottom of their skirts and these were edged with beads of various colors. Most of them displayed tinkling ornaments made from tufts of deer's hair, dyed red, and placed in small pieces of tin. Their energetic movements were accompanied by the musical sound of tinkling bells.

Most of the bread was made with cornmeal in the usual way, but today they also are baking a special bread made of green corn.

The green corn has been cut from the cob, and pounded in a mortar until it's as thick as whipped cream. Lightly salted, they have poured it onto some corn leaves in a long oblong mold. It is baking in the ashes of the fire—a gourmet's delight.

Dinner will be served in wooden bowls or on wooden slabs, according to the guest's preference and their availability. Each guest will use his own knife to cut the meat which he will hold in his fingers. There are a few pewter spoons which the hostesses will give to the party of chiefs and elders. In their structured society the honored guests will sit directly in front of the fire altar which is on a high mound in the center of this natural Plymouth amphi-theater.

The squaws know that some guests will have their own spoons. They also have provided small wooden scoops for the children. Before dawn they brought several kegs of rum and one large barrel of whiskey which they have taken great pains to conceal from their guests until after the feast.

Looking around the assemblage we can see several Ottawa wrapped in their gaudy blankets. Under the pine is a group of half-naked Ojibwa with their brightly-painted tomahawks keeping time to the music of the drum which is softly signalling the beginning of the feast.

In spite of the varied costumes, all these people know they are Algonkian. They understand each other's dialect and read the same totem. They share the same traditions; worship the same Great Spirit. Among the Potowatomi are many cross-cousins who have never denied their kinship to the others.

The researcher finds many interesting affiliations, but they are difficult to trace. For example, these proud half-naked Ojibwa call themselves "Anishinabe" which roughly translated means "first man" or "original man." Perhaps they were the first of their kind! The "Pots" call them Ojibwa. The French at the Fort called them Chippewa or Saulters.

The Ojibwa (sometimes spelled Ojibway) or Chippewa were one of the "Three Fires" who divided at Mackinac centuries ago. Plymouth's Chief Tonquish always made his mark on the treaties he signed as a Chippewa, but he is believed to have been part Potowatomi, as was his surviving wife.

The name Algonquian is derived from Algomequin, and it means "people across the river." About six hundred years ago the "Three Fires" were one tribe living on the north shore of the St. Lawrence river and the Atlantic ocean. At one time their territory extended from the Rocky Mountains to Labrador, and from upper Manitoba to North Carolina. The Michigan Ojibwa are descendants of that far-flung Canadian tribe.

The Michigan Ojibwa have camped along the river north of the Fort at Detroit since time immemorial. Independent, proud, different from the others—a race apart. They were not easily approached even by the white missionaries. Somehow they have the look of eagles. It is as though they vaguely remember a long flight—another time—another world. It is a fact that some Ojibwa have a different way of measuring time and space.

5. Old Shaman of the Tonquish Faces Governor of Territory

Alone on his tired, little Indian pony, limping along Pontiac's ancient trail, the last Shaman (medicine man) of the Tonquish Potowatomi pondered his plight.

Yesterday a paleface governor of this territory had tried to buy the Shaman's influence; tried to force him to direct his people's thoughts toward a new land in the far west. The paleface had threatened much and promised little, and the old Shaman was greatly worn by the pressure of his own conflicting thoughts.

Near the intersection of the Grand River trail and the path to Silver Lake, an area known today as New Hudson, he turned his pony eastward toward the white settlements. He wanted to see what had happened to his old stamping ground along the Middle Rouge.

The Shaman had heard of many changes there. Other duties had kept him away from Tonquish Plain for almost six months. Now, in December 1819, he was responding to the call of Toga's people to install their new chief.

Because he was one of the most celebrated medicine men among both the Ojibwa and the Potowatomi, the Shaman recognized his commitment, his obligation, to his Tonquish cousins. He promised himself that he would not fail them. But the path was long and rough, and both he and the pony were exceedingly weary.

After almost an hour's slow riding he turned southeast toward Plymouth Mound. At a crosspath known today as Baseline (Eight Mile) and Novi Roads, he was startled to hear the clanging noise of chains being dragged along the ground.

Alighting quickly, he crept behind a thicket close to the laboring surveyors. He saw them signaling each other. How strange, he thought. What are they doing? They are peering through that box at some imaginary bird or tree. Perhaps that's the way they measure. And they are pounding stakes into good Mother Earth. Bonga! Bonga! Bonga! Damn it all.

With the treaty of Detroit in 1807, and subsequent agreements including the Treaty of 1815, the Indians in the Plymouth-Canton and surrounding area had ceded much of their Michigan land to the Americans.

The white man's new boundary ran due north from Fort Defiance, Ohio, to a line designated as the principal Michigan meridian, a few miles east of what now is Lansing. This is Lansing's Meridian Road.

The base line was run east about eight miles north of Fort Detroit. Base Line Road is derived from this, and it also is known as Eight Mile Road.

From these two lines (Meridian and Base Line) surveyors established all the townships in Michigan including those in the Upper Peninsula.

The box which mystified the Shaman was a hand-held compass housed in a wooden frame. The surveyors could get a straight line by aligning the protruding sights in the box with their old-fashioned mercury compass. The noisy chain which had startled the Indian was a standard Gunther chain of 100 links of eight inches each. It was supposed to be, and usually was, exactly 66 feet long.

Bonga! Bonga! The old Shaman looked at the sun and knew he must hurry if he was to reach Plymouth Mound before noon.

Along the Middle Rouge near Northville he again was startled to see two new mills grinding the white man's corn. And there were several cabins along the familiar stream which had not been there before. He wondered what had happened to his people's weirs and traps. They must be stolen by now, he concluded.

Urging the little pony on toward Plymouth Mound, the Shaman continued to brood about his confrontation with the white governor. In his heart he questioned the white man's promises. "Oh, Great Spirit, what do I do now?" he cried aloud.

Suddenly, in his anguish, he was transfixed with the foreboding that he would never ride this way again. This thought came to him as in a dream. But it was a true thought and he recognized its truth.

Those among the Shaman's followers who really knew him sensed that his perceptions were unique; his prescience was remarkable and not unlike that of a few other survivors of the Ojibwa of ancient lineage. He lived alone and somewhat apart from the usual rhythm of time and place. His people never doubted him and their confidence was the mainstay of his extensive and successful medical practice. He was the most successful healer in this part of Michigan and consulted by Indians and whites alike.

After awhile his intimate confrontation with his private world evoked a prayer.

Of course, I have no idea of exactly what he said, but I have read hundreds of Indian prayers and I am sure that his petition was not unlike this prayer which I have written:

"Hey-a-a. Hey-a-a. Hey-a-a.
I am a poor old Shaman, Oh, Great Spirit
The last of my people. Hear me.
Oh, hear me.

I cry for my people.
They have given their land away.
Hey-a-a. Hey-a-a.
Help us now, oh, Great Spirit.
Help us to find our way into the West.
I have been trying to believe
the white man's promises.
I have been seeking them,
but I cannot find them.
We did not ask these people here.

Oh, Great Spirit. Where are their promises
now?
Where are we now? What have we done
to cause us to depart from our homeland?
We really have no place to go.
Where is our ancient dream?
Forsake us not, Beloved Spirit,
Be with us now. Guide us now.
Hey-a-a. Hey-a-a. Hey-a-a.

As his prayer blended with the wind he felt his own tears falling down his craggy cheeks. But soon his depressed spirit was lifted by the sound of the drumbeat on Plymouth Mound.

Now, he said to himself, I must paint on a happier face.

41

They trust me and depend upon me. I am their Shaman—their teacher. I must not let them down, yet they must never know the price of my bravery.

When the sun reached high noon he strode among the assembled throng with every appearance of poise and power. He wore his favorite mask and his most elegant robe, and he walked with an air of majesty most becoming to the head Shaman of the mystical order of the Mediwiwin.

Bowing graciously to the magnificent Powotomi altar, his powerful voice and magical words hypnotized them into the belief that he had secret, esoteric knowledge of all the mysteries on their Indian earth.

The murmuring crowd of nearly 200 sat on the ground in ever-widening concentric circles around their impressive altar. At the sight of the Shaman they suddenly were silent.

Some had walked long distances to hear him and they did not want to miss a word. They longed to hear his marvelous voice telling them that all was yet right in their world. They believed he could restore their peace and preserve their pride. He could make their hearts sing again like a bird in the forest at the dawn's first light.

6. Conflict Divides Tribe at Chief Tonga's Installation

There was a hint of snow in the air on that December day in 1819, as though the winds of winter were about to begin again. But the sun shone brightly on Plymouth Mound, warming the crowd of almost 200.

Many in the crowd came from long distances to witness the installation of the successor to the late lamented Chief Tonquish. When the sun signalled high noon on Tonquish Plain, an insistent drum beat began, and the murmuring crowd quickly became silent and watchful.

When the drum sounded, the tribe's old Shaman (medicine man) strode forth to conduct the ritual ceremony. The Shaman was garbed in a magnificent, old-style robe of painted skins with an elaborate, beaded girdle and a heavily ornamented neckpiece. His head was crowned with a beautiful, golden cap decorated with eagle feathers. His wrinkled old face was covered with the mask of the Metai, symbolizing his chiefdom in the mystical order of Indian medicine men. Among the Potowatomi and others, including the Ojibwa and the Huron, this order was widely respected. It was known as the Mediwiwin.

Watching intently, the hushed crowd saw their Shaman move energetically and without pause to the center of their concentric circles where he faced the altar.

The watchers observed that a small fire of no great consequence was slumbering in the altar's firepot. Without any special prayer, or any recognition of the crowd, or any statement of his purpose or of the purpose for which they were assembled, the Shaman simply faced the altar.

Then slowly and somewhat majestically he raised his right hand toward high heaven as though he would invoke the blessing of their gods upon the fire. He then passed his left hand over the firepot and instantly a large and powerful flame burst forth. The crowd, enchanted by this evidence of the Shaman's "magic," erupted with loud appreciative cheers.

"Huzza! Huzza! Huzza! Wa hoo! Wa hoo!" and so forth. Their enthusiasm seemed boundless. With their approval still ringing in his ears, the old Shaman moved quickly to tap Telonga on the shoulder. He directed Telonga to accompany him in a processional around the altar.

Together Telonga, or Tonga as he was commonly called, and the Shaman with his right hand on Tonga's left shoulder, walked slowly about the altar. As they walked a drum beat in the distance sounded very softly while the Shaman kept in a constant whispered contact with Tonga. The tone was confidential, and the soft voice was not audible to even the first row of circles. While the Shaman was instructing Tonga, the young chief seemed to be respectful and obedient. In fact, his young supporters in the crowd were amazed at the conformity Tonga displayed, and some were worried for fear he had been entrapped by the mysticism of the old guard.

What the Shaman said was probably the usual ritual for the installation of an important chief. This ceremony had been handed down for hundreds of years. The exact knowledge of its content is a closely guarded secret and in many generations—perhaps a thousand years—not once has its basic content ever become public knowledge.

When Tonga and the Shaman had circled the altar three times, they returned to the fire which had died down somewhat but still was a visible blaze.

Taking Tonga's right hand in his, the Shaman passed it over the fire and once again an enormous flame, larger than the first, burst forth to astound the assemblage. Then, following whispered instructions, Tonga raised his right hand toward the sky to indicate the source of his new power.

This gesture was greeted with a few polite "Huzza's" but, for the most part, a respectful silence fell upon the crowd. They were awaiting the Shaman's good words which would comfort them and give them hope. While they waited, several "peace" pipes were passed around the circles. Braves and squaws alike were taking big drafts from the familiar pipe.

With the handsome, young Chief Tonga standing respectfully by his side, the Shaman's powerful voice filled the amphitheater with the confident, hopeful tones the crowd had long respected and admired. The Shaman was eloquent and fervent in his praise of the many favors the Great Spirit had granted his children in the past.

He told them to remember that once the Great Spirit had given them a vast land stretching from sun to sun. From the "frozen sea of the North to the warm waters of the South—this land is our land," he asserted.

"Today we will feast on the bounty of this generous land. Although it would seem that in recent years we have fallen from favor with the Great Spirit, I will promise you that our time will come yet again," he continued, "the paleface will disappear, and we will reclaim our heritage. Today the returning favor of the Great Spirit has brought us a brave and bright new chief who will guide us to the promised land."

This ominous statement seemed to startle Tonga, and he pulled away from the Shaman. It was evident that the only "promised land" Tonga wanted was Plymouth Mound. Noting this the Shaman hurriedly finished his speech with, "Here is Telonga. I name him your new chief."

Instantly the crowd burst forth into prolonged cheering. They were about to begin a dance in celebration of Tonga's election when the Shaman, red-faced and angry, commanded them to be quiet.

Making his voice heard above the noisy throng, he said: "I bring you yet another blessing. Today I bring you boundless new hunting grounds. In the far, far west beyond the troubled waters of the paleface there is a vast land of plenty. The Great Spirit will not allow the paleface to enter there. We have been promised this land in the West. I believe that promise, and I have come to walk with you there."

Suddenly the Shaman stumbled and Telonga broke his fall and let him rest gently on the old stones of the altar.

Then in his own right, Telonga addressed the crowd with: "My beloved brothers, I would walk with you here. For I say to you, the paleface does not own this land, nor is it ours to give. It is our land and their land. It belongs to the Great Spirit who does not divide, who is always the same, whose bounty knows no limits.

"The sun that shines on us now, shines on all. The birds that sing, the corn that grows, is the same for all. The grass is not greener in the West, nor is the corn richer, nor the deer larger. We have it right here. We must make our peace with the paleface, and we must teach him to respect our treaty rights."

7. Treaties Terminate Indian Ownership In Our Area

A great Miami chief, Little Turtle, who was born in 1752 and died in 1812, once said, according to the old records, "My fathers kindled the first fire at Detroit."

He added that their camps extended along the river to the Maumee, and down the Scio to and the Ohio to the Wabash, then on to "She-gog-ong" (Chicago).

There is no reason to doubt him. There was a Miami village at Detroit as late as 1703, and evidence that it was a remnant of a much larger and older Miami village. The Miami were a leading tribe.

The Detroit area also was home to the great Ottowa Chief Pontiac and his nephew Okemos.

Their headquarters was on Peche Island in Lake St. Clair. Other tribes criss-crossed our area. Many Ottowa and the Chippewa called Wayne and Oakland counties home.

South of the Rouge was home base for the Wyandot and the Huron. And, in the central area perhaps as far east as Saline was a strange group called Mascoutens. Not too much is known about them. Around Saginaw there was a tribe of Sauks, and the Foxes lived in the St. Clair area.

Some readers have requested a map to "locate the Indians." This is not possible because we are dealing with roving, migratory people who were in an unsettled state. They preferred the free life of the hunter although there is evidence that before the advent of the white man there was some stability to the Indian's home place. Tonquish was more stable and appears to have always centered his activities in this part of Wayne County.

The tribes and their trails mingled and intermingled and, while respecting each other's totem and family lines and obeying their own ancestral creeds, they traded and bartered with each other.

The Chippewa, Potowatomi and Ottowa were Algonquin and understood each other's dialect. The Foxes seemed to be allied with the Sauk. They both were Algonquin as were the Miami and the Mascouten. The Wyandot and the Huron were of Iroquoian stock as were the Mahicans.

From the earliest time intermarriage was not uncommon among these people. Little Turtle's mother, who lived on the bay of the Maumee, was a Mahican. Chief Pontiac's mother was an Ojibwa. There were Shawnees among the Tonquish.

The early treaty maps are the most reliable indicators of Indian villages.

After the surveyors laid out Eight Mile Road, we can pinpoint the Treaty of 1807's exact location of Chief Tonquish's village, but expecting to find him there is wishful thinking.

Tonquish, like the others, roamed at will and followed the hunt for food. And Tonquish, like the others, did not willingly relinquish possession of his freedom.

Many treaties with the Indian were for the "extinquishing of titles," and Tonquish and all the other Indian chiefs of that era did not appear to take seriously the process of "touching the pen" or "marking their X" to the white man's document. So the "extinguishing process" for clearing titles had to be repeated over and over again.

Wayne and Washtenaw counties, for instance, were bargained for at least four times. The Treaty of Detroit, 1807, which Chief Tonquish "signed" was the fourth purchase that was made of Wayne, Washtenaw, Macomb, Oakland, Genesee, Lapeer, St. Clair, Livingston counties and large portions of Sanilac, Tuscola, Shiawasee, Ingham and Jackson counties.

This area had been controlled by the Potowatomi, Chippewa, Ottowa, and Wyandot or Huron. Although they unconditionally ceded their lands, they were most reluctant to relinquish possession.

Chief Tonquish, for example, was known for his haughty, proud attitude. He appeared to believe that everything in his territory belonged to him regardless of treaties. His attempt to appropriate some of the settler's goods caused his death. At this late date, most of the evidence has disappeared, but we can safely assume that Tonquish was not alone in his assumption of power.

Treaty signing was regarded by the Indians as a festive occasion.

The white man brought plenty of liquor, and there were hoards of dishonest traders with cheap beads and overpriced merchandise which the Indian freely purchased.

Tonquish received $400 for his land in the Treaty of Detroit ceremony on Nov. 17, 1807. It is doubtful if much of that money found its way back to his impoverished clan.

Article Six of this treaty granted Tonquish "two sections of one mile square each" near Tonquish's village on the river Rouge. This area runs to where the Rouge crosses Grand River Avenue (not far from where the trail marker is on

Shiawasee Road in Farmington) to some miles south of the Nankin Mills area.

The Tonquish burial marker on Wayne Road near Joy is in an area owned by him. When Tonquish was fleeing up the Rouge toward Nankin Mills he was headed for home.

Other signatories to the 1807 document include Chippewa chiefs Peewanshe me nogh, and MaMau-she qua ta or "Bad Legs." Ottowa chiefs Aubauway and Kawackewan also signed the document as well as Tonquish. Among the Potowatomies was the mark of Tonquish, Noname, Nawme, Ninewa and Skash. Sounds like a law firm in the Penobscot building!

The truth is these Indians had no concept of land ownership or property rights in the white man's sense. Ceding their land and getting drunk at a treaty pow-wow was easy, but relinquishing possession was not so easy.

They had hunted this area since time immemorial. Many of them roamed a thousand miles over the Middle West in their hunting forays, and they freely shared this privilege with the others. They were obliged to spend their lives in a constant search for food and in an avoidance of death by enemies or by accident.

No born-free Indian will sign away his homeland forever. Like Tonquish, they kept running until they were caught and they kept on fighting until they were dead.

Occasionally an Indian would catch on to the white man's technique in land appropriation.

There is a story, perhaps apocryphal, of an old Sauk who lived on the bay near Sauk-in-naw (Saginaw). The American traders knew that the Sauks were much weakened by warfare and that their chief had urged them to leave the area.

The white settlers were pressuring them to sell out. Our old Sauk had control of several hundred acres on the bay

51

and he was determined to hang on to it. When a trader came to his hut one morning and offered $25 for the land, the Indian said, "Fine, OK. If my squaw agree, we go."

Then he had a private conference with his squaw and returned with "She no go unless you pay her $25 too." A fierce argument ensued, but the old Indian was determined and immovable, so the trader parted with another $25.

This story may be the first indication of a pioneer spirit of woman's rights in Saginaw County. More probably it is a good indication that the Indians were beginning to learn how to deal with the white man.

The Sauks, who also were Algonquin, were found in Michigan but were much more numerous in Wisconsin. The Potowatomi, the Ottowa, and the Chippewa-Ojibwa did not seem to like them much.

When Black Hawk, a Sauk, raised his rebellion known as the Black Hawk War most of the members of the "Three Fires Confederation" refused to join him. This doomed his rebellion from the start.

The reason for this enmity is lost in the shroud of history and may never be brought to light. But it is a fact that the old Sauk trail which began along the Raisin River was Sauk on the west bank only. No respectable "Pot" would step foot on a Sauk tread mark. So the old trail was Potowatomi on the east bank and Sauk on the west.

8. New Chicago Turnpike Follows Ancient Indian Trail Marks

Among the many notable achievements of Father Gabriel Richard, priest of Ste. Anne's at Fort Detroit, was the procuring of an appropriation from a reluctant Congress for the development of the schools and the roads of the new Michigan Territory.

Father Richard, an elected delegate to Congress in 1824, persuaded the government to provide funds for building a road through the wilderness between Detroit and Chicago.

The new turnpike was to follow the old Potowatomi Trail. Ten years under construction, when it was finally completed in 1834, a most enthusiastic celebration marked the event.

Actually the road was nothing to brag about.

Passable only during the dry season, a rainy spell would leave the travellers stranded in the wilderness at the mercy of Indians and bears alike. But the road was a great boon to the settlers and traders who were pushing into the Michigan Territory.

Today we call this old "Potowatomi Trail" Michigan Avenue or U.S. 12. It has taken a back seat now to our super highway I-94.

While the road building was going on negotiations with the Indians were proceeding at a faster pace. Treaty followed treaty leaving a trail of forlorn hopes and broken promises. The ramifications of all these negotiations, the lies and chicanery, the base trickery, are too gruesome to relate. It is another depressing story of man's inhumanity to man.

For ten long years from 1824 on, the road building never ceased. The Potowatomi and their friends, the Huron and the Wyandotte, and other tribes in the area were pushed back from their familiar trail as the noisy chains of the surveyors pursued their relentless course.

The quiet of the wilderness was broken by the din of raucous road gangs, while the beautiful, primitive forest succumbed log by log. Within the decade, except for isolated Indian enclaves, the white man's cabins replaced the Indian homes along the Trail. The year 1827 marked the last, large Indian encampment in this area.

The last encampment occurred on the old John Geddes farm in a place where today Geddes Road meets the Huron River.

Eight years have gone by since Chief Tonquish and his son were shot. The Indian world Tonquish knew has been changed forever.

Pertinent to this summary of these old events is the fact that Plymouth's Chief Tonquish made his mark on some of the early treaties. After the Tonquish deaths, the area seemed to be represented by Tonga and by Chief Leopold Pokagon. Pokagon was second in rank to Topenebee, a famous Indian chief who was the supreme chief of all the Potowatomi, If we would know the fate of the Tonquish group we must explore the Pokagon clan. Leopold Pokagon assisted in the ceremony that installed Telonga, the successor to Chief Tonquish. In times of trouble the Tonquish were taken under Pokagon's protective wing.

Another interesting sidelight which helps us to understand these early Indians is to explore their social structure as it pertains to their relationships with each other.

Many books have been written on this involved subject. It is so complicated that it is difficult to summarize briefly; however, the kinship system was a way of life to the Potowatomi and to many other Indians of the Algonquin blood.

It is significant that the practice of systematically marrying someone in the social category of a cross-cousin resulted in a kinship system in which there are many relatives by marriage. This system protected the totem, the family lineage, and yet it also banned marriage among close kin so any element of incest was avoided. It can be explained more easily by illustration.

For example, Chief Leopold Pokagon's first wife was a daughter of Sawak, who was Chief Topenebee's brother and hunting companion. Topenebee died in 1840 after more than forty years as supreme chief of all the Potowatomi of Michigan, Indiana, Illinois and Wisconsin. To successfully control such a large group for four decades required very superior ability and political know-how.

To assist him in the management of this loosely-knit tribe Topenebee not only had the convenient aid of the kinship system but he also maintained a group of fishing and hunting pals, a kind of "kitchen cabinet." Among them were lesser chiefs including Shavehead, Weesaw, Pokagon, and, to some extent Tonquish. There were many cross-cousin links within this governing group.

Acuarie, Pokagon's first wife, also had great status among the group as Sawak's sister and a most successful medicine

55

Leopold Pokagon, by Van Sanden. A chief from the Saint Joseph River, Pokagon and his followers remained on their small farms in Michigan and were not removed to the west. *Courtesy Northern Indiana Historical Society.*

woman. Chief Weesaw, a prominent member of the "kitchen cabinet," was Topenebee's brother. Topenebee's father, Aniquiba, owned thousands of acres in western Michigan. His headquarters were where the city of Niles now stands. As the crescendo of the road builders was echoing through their forest the Indians drew closer together within the protective bonds of their kinship system.

Chief Leopold Pokagon made several moves toward the assimilation of the Potowatomi into white society. His keen mind perceived that their security and future lay in that direction. He was supported in this by many wholesome, Christian forces within the government of the United States.

The Office of Indian Affairs feared that the Potowatomis were acquiring all of the white vices while "rejecting the virtues of Christian civilization."

Thomas McKenney, Superintendent of Indian Affairs and long a champion of assimiliation, changed after a tour in 1827 and became a most powerful advocate of Indian removal.

McKenney told the Congress that the Indians were not becoming farmers as had been hoped, but were spending their time "hunting, catching fish, planting patches of corn, getting drunk, fighting and often starving." To save the Indians from "complete debauchery" the politicians recommended that they be removed beyond the Mississippi where they could pursue their traditional way of life.

Chief Pokagon objected strenuously to these conclusions and made several trips to Fort Detroit to enlist the aid of Father Gabriel Richard. Pokagon made a personal appeal directly to Father Richard who sent a priest, Frederick Reze, to establish a school at Pokagon's village in Bertrand Township, Berrien County. Reze baptized Pokagon, who was about 55 and his wife who was 46. Many members of the band, including Chief Telonga, joined in the ceremony and were baptized at this time.

Perhaps some of these Indians were motivated by blind obedience to their chief; others were making sincere efforts to try to get along in the white man's world. The church and school at Bertrand prospered and became very important. But there was a pagan element within many tribes that would never surrender in their thought or their will to the idea of white supremacy. This group never embraced the church. And it has been alleged that this group, a small minority, performs pagan rites to this very day.

9. Culture Changes Evident Among Dispossessed Indian Tribes

Among the John Askin papers at the Burton Library in Detroit is the transcript of a deed dated Feb. 28, 1773. The area involved marked the site of the Potowatomi Fort Detroit Settlement.

It is reasonable to assume that some of the Tonquish group were involved in these negotiations because later the same people appear to be associated with Chief Tonquish.

The deed states that these Potowatomi ceded their lands to one "Robert Navarre, the younger" and provided "forever that he may cultivate the same, light a fire thereon and take care of our dead."

Their faith in Navarre's ability to save this Golgotha from desecration seems, indeed, pathetic as well as naive. But in 1773 what other options did they have? At that date all the Indians in the Detroit area were encircled by the powerful white man. Even Pontiac's people were leaving their sanctuary on Peche Island just north of Belle Isle. All were under pressure to move westward. Concealing their beautiful black altar in their Shaman's ceremonial robe, the chief and his people moved out to a favorite fishing area, the fork of the Rouge near Farmington.

Later the Treaty of 1807 granted Chief Tonquish two sections of one mile square each near this area of the Rouge which the treaty makers designated as "Tonquish Village." The Indians of this clan claimed hunting, fishing and trapping privileges over an even larger area, including Northville, Plymouth, Canton, Livonia, Farmington and Redford. Their old chief thought he owned Tonquish Plain, regardless of the treaty, and he fought and died there.

While this struggle for survival was going on, Detroit was growing by leaps and bounds.

In 1817, in an effort to improve the well-traveled Woodbridge Street, local road builders uncovered several dozen Indian graves. They were found on Navarre's old farm near what is today Navarre Place and Woodbridge Street.

It is probable that these Potowatomi were buried according to the usual customs of their tribe. When Tonquish heard of this desecration he must have been enraged.

Professor George Quimby of the University of Chicago, in his estimable little book "Indian Life in the Upper Great Lakes," said that the Potowatomi and the Ottowa as well as other Algonquin had a system of organized rituals and practices which involved belief in a "Great Spirit." They also believed that the human body had but one soul which, after death, found its way to heaven. To the Potowatomi, heaven was a trail over the rainbow, beyond the Milky Way, to a somewhere in the far, far West.

So it was serious business when the Tonquish Potowatomi extracted a solemn promise from Navarre to keep a fire burning in their graveyard. Fire was an essential part of their ritual. They were known as the "fire people," and the light of the fire was needed so that the Chibiabos (in Potowatomi, this meant the escort to heaven) could find them.

Religion and medicine were closely related in the Indian world. Both religion and medicine were, to the Indian mind, involved with "magic." To them, all things, animate and inanimate, were permeated by a force that had the power to influence or control one's life. If one had good luck one must pay homage to this mystic force. If one fell ill, the misfortune was caused by some "evil spirit." Then the Shaman, or medicine man, must be called in to help ward off the evil.

The Woodbridge Street grave site contained several loaded flintlock rifles as well as beaded bullet pouches with extra flints. Many iron axes also were found. Quinby said that a brave's grave might contain "white clay tobacco pipes made in Scotland, silver armbands, gorgets, and ear ornaments made in London or Montreal, a glass bottle of peppermint oil for his stomach, made in France, and a flint and steel 'strike-a-light' made in Boston." There was usually punk for starting fires, pewter dishes of food for the long journey over the rainbow, powdered vermillion for face paint, and many other unique items they deemed necessary for a good life in the next world.

An Indian woman's grave often contained her brass kettle, several brooches, necklaces of colored glass beads, bracelets and ear bobs, blue china, white porcelain, Staffordshire teacups, a mirror, a jew's-harp, and other furnishings considered necessary to her happiness.

All of these items are indicative of their changing culture and their growing participation in the white man's trade world. Unfortunately, by 1830 the animal skins which provided the wherewithal for the Indian's trade were vanishing from this area. The product of the hunt, which was the staple of their diet as well as their trade, came to an end about the same time the push for Indian land greatly intensified. This transition clearly is shown in the excavations of mounds and funeral tombs in our area.

According to professor W.B. Hindsale, The University of Michigan, in his excellent booklet "The Indians of Washtenaw County," some of the mounds along Geddes Road in the vicinity of Concordia College contained flint, deer horn ornaments, shell beads and the usual Algonquin-type burial items.

But the Dexter mound, which dates after this period, contained nothing but human bones—evidence of a culture in transition and of a people being pushed out of their familiar habitat. Today's Detroit, built on the fires of the old, covers many a unique Indian treasure.

When Tonquish and the Potowatomi set up their black altar on Plymouth Mound they were bowing not only to a sacred trust, but they were paying homage to an idea that goes back in their culture to the beginning of time. This is the fire theme, and the snake that was carved on the base of the altar is part of that theme.

This theme appears in many other Indian cultures, particularly the Mayan and the Aztec. The Adena-Hopewell people, who built the largest snake mound in the world in Ohio—a serpentine monster that extends over several acres—also made gorgeous textiles and rugs more than 2,000 years ago. Like the Potowatomies, the Hopewell Indians were great corn growers. The feast of green corn was well-established among them.

In the Grand River Valley of Michigan there probably are five dozen Hopewell burial mounds, some of them not yet excavated.

Let us return to our main theme—the Potowatomi of Tonquish vintage and the story of their struggle for survival. There are a number of other significant facts to be considered. No tribe in the Middle west "signed" more treaties than our Potowatomi. The first "signing" with the United States occurred in 1789, and the last in 1872.

The Potowatomi were parties to forty-seven treaties. After the War of 1812 a series of negotiations nibbled away at their territory, chunk by chunk. When it was over, they had no more land to give away.

(These treaties may be found in Charles J. Kappler's edition of "Indian Laws and Treaties," published by Washington's Indian Affairs Department. I found this book in the Graduate School Library at The University of Michigan. The Clement Library, also on the Michigan campus and the Bentley Library on the North Campus, are excellent sources of information.)

September 1833 marked a traumatic turning point in the lives of these Potowatomi. Let's look at the scene. According to several writers of that day, Shecagon was a small, dirty, unhealthy village of wretched wooden hovels, a few feet high, barely clearing a sodden woodland.

Washed by the winds of Lake Mishigum, it was home to hundreds of "birds of passage." Law and order was represented by the tired, old and battered Fort Dearborn and a few, less than a hundred, militia. Near the fort dwelt land speculators and horse thieves, rogues of every description.

As Charles Latrobe, a young English traveler of that time, said in his admirable "The Rambler in North America," the town was full of "halfbreeds, quarter-breeds, white, black, brown, and red, and men of no breed at all." Some dealt in pigs, poultry, and potatoes. Some lied when they posed as creditors of the tribe, and some were grog sellers. Others were Indian agents and traders—"sharpers of every degree."

Chicago was a chaos—mired in muck, rubbish and crime. What hope is there for the survivors among the Tonquish? Will these thieving, lying rascals take all their treaty money and will their downfall (whiskey) take the rest?

10. She-gog-on Streets Awash With Debris

A strange wind blew off Lake Mishigum that morning in September 1833. It was violent and dangerous, and carried with it a fierce undertow which almost drowned several unwary braves who were fishing in the bay.

The waves roared right into the dirty She-gog-on streets making them awash with their own debris. There was no harbor, no breakwater, and the river flowed directly into the lake.

At night the sound of the pounding surf echoed for blocks along the dismal streets of hovels and rooming houses, dirty saloons, and unkempt trading posts.

When the dawn broke the storm had spent itself; the morning sun shone upon one of the most colorful sights in the world—an encampment of about 5,000 Algonquin-Potowatomi, Chippewa, and Ottawa in their gorgeous pow-wow regalia.

The little village, a tawdry frontier outpost at best, held together by the militia at old Fort Dearborn, was completely surrounded this September day. On every side as far as eyes could see were Indian camps.

On the flat prairie beyond the village were row after row of tipi and wigwams, many bearing the insignia or totem of a clan.

There was the Turtle clan, and over there were the symbols of the Hare; further to the west, the Eagle group. So they kept themselves together but separate.

Beyond the village in the woods near the lake were hundreds more. It was so crowded that the latecomers were camping on the dunes of the beach. The cacophonous dissonance of their dialectal differences, and their strenuous efforts to understand each other in spite of these differences, turned the scene into a veritable Tower of Babel.

The Michigan Potowatomi under the leadership of Chief Leopold Pokagon had drawn an ideal camping spot at the lake near the edge of the woods.

Leopold and his good wife Elizabeth, who was a relative of Chief Tonquish, had been assigned to this preferred spot.

The Pokagons were christianized Indians who had visited Father Gabriel Richard many years before, and through their intercession a church had been established for their clan in Betrand Township, Berrien County. Pokagon's brilliant son, Simon, was attending college at the fledgling, little backwoods school that became the University of Notre Dame.

Simon was to become chief of the tribe one day, and a student and world traveler, an author of several remarkable books, and a poet widely respected here and abroad.

Simon Pokagon was a brilliant man who spoke five languages and was regarded as the best educated Indian in the world. Recondite and profound—a man who commanded respect, from white and Indian alike.

Let us return to Chicago where pandemonium reigns.

Look at the mob in the street! There must be a thousand young braves in that wild throng. Their revelry was born of futility. According to John Caton, a young lawyer who witnessed the spectacle, the noisy din was made by "beating on hollow vessels" and "striking sticks and clubs together."

66

The richly costumed braves danced along the bank of the river on the north side, "stopping in front of every house they passed to perform." Caton added that they "finally crossed the north branch of the river and proceeded along the west side of the south branch to the vicinity of the present Lake Street, where they danced in front of the Sauganash Hotel.

Most reporters of that era say that they continued down Lake Street to the Exchange Coffee House where they danced again. Then to the Tremont House Hotel where a number of white women appeared at the windows. The Indians brandished their war clubs quite merrily, howling with delight at the terror they created. The women quickly bolted their doors, terrified at the prospect of imminent death.

The column of young warriors continued on to Fort Dearborn where they performed for the men of the garrison. More sophisticated than the women of the hotels, the officers knew that they were watching a farewell.

The officers and their men knew what every sentient Indian knew that this was not a celebration but a dance to commemorate the customs of their ancestors. It was a dance of death and all Chicago rocked with its convulsions.

That evening a familiar face pitched his wigwam near the Pokagons. What a wonderful surprise!

It was the wrinkled, old craggy-faced Shaman of the Tonquish. He was delayed by the storm, he said. He was too proud to tell the truth, that he had to proceed at a snail's pace because he was almost too old to travel from his home along the river in Cass County, Mich. He was warmly greeted by the Pokagons who helped him establish his wigwam and gave him food for his evening meal.

"A bad omen," the Shaman kept muttering, a "very bad omen." What are you talking about?, Leopold inquired. "That storm means the Great Spirit is protesting," Shaman replied. "Spirit no like Chemokemon's tricks. You watch out for tricks, Pokagon. I not sleep 'til you promise."

And so Leopold assured him that he would be alert to the Chemokemon's schemes. (Chemokemon to these Indians meant the man with the long knife, the white man. It is a fiction that the Indians of this era called the white man "pale face." This is a myth from some Daniel Boone movie, but it is not historically true. In the Indian sign language and in the spoken language and in the picture writing the name used for white man was not "pale face" but "man-with-a-hat-on.")

It had taken many weeks for them to assemble. They had come from Michigan, Illinois, Wisconsin, Indiana, Ohio, Ontario—from seemingly everywhere. Old Hickory's agents had convinced them there would be plenty of free food, meat and whiskey for all furnished by the government. There was a lot these Indians did not know about the great, white father in Washington (Andrew Jackson) but they were to learn soon enough about the price of this "free whiskey."

Charles J. Latrobe, a young traveler who witnessed the parley, spoke of Indians singing and chanting every night.

The light of the camp fires illuminated their gaily painted faces. The Indians raced their ponies down the muddy streets and every wigwam you "peak into" reported Latrobe, you may witness the chief sitting in dogged silence while the women argued over gift trifles."

Sometimes the women were more saturated with the fumes of whiskey than the braves. From some tents you could hear wild laughter, and others were quiet and orderly. It was a very human drama.

Under every bush were old warriors, smoking and pow-wowing, drinking and lying to each other about their heroic past. Many a wildly exaggerated tale of fishing and hunting

68

and, most of all, of getting the best of the Chemokemon, regaled the campfires far into the night.

The women and children who had come with their braves were delighted with the arrangements because they didn't have to cook. There was plenty of food and it was free. So the squaws spent their days gossiping, enjoying their friends, and a few got into mischief.

Chicago was filled with a carnival spirit. Some of these women were truly beautiful and their colorful costumes emphasized their exotic beauty. They were fair game for some of the louts who infested the village at night.

Professor Grant Foreman in his fascinating study, "The Last Trek of the Indians," discusses the logistics of feeding several thousand Indians for six weeks, and it was tremendous.

There were hundreds of traders and merchants, many drivers in carts coming and going, farmers and folk singers, courtesans and concubines. Everything was in Chicago that September 1833.

Foreman lists some of the bills of the so-called "merchants." And some actually delivered their merchandise at outrageous prices yet in compliance with treaty terms. The bills were audited in Washington and paid by government agents. No doubt many of these bills were loaded and fraudulent. Perhaps some were not.

From a historian's viewpoint the trading records are noteworthy. Foreman cites the Senate Record (Document 512 of the First Session of the Twenty-third Congress of the United States).

After their practical needs were met by rifles, shotguns, ducking guns; beaver, otter, and muskrat traps; awls and gimlets; camp kettles; powder and lead; bridles and saddles, including "plush" saddles; shoes; sewing silk; ticking;

combs; "silver-mounted spurs" and gun flints, gun linsey, stripes, prints, cloaks, satinet; tablespoons and shears; blankets and hose; "superfine cloth of various hues," crepe, calico, ginghams; fancy morocco trunks, snuffboxes; and scores of jew's-harps. Then came adornment: Four dozen cock feathers and six dozen foxtails were needed.

There was an endless list of shawls including: Indian shawls, chintz, scarlet cashmere, crepe, turkey-red, Prussian, Valencia, French, Thibet, Palmyra, and Circassian. Thousand of yards of piece goods and an endless variety of cloaks including "camlet, Spanish, and silk Circassian."

The abstract fills 490 pages of which at least 150 refers to items ordered by the Potowatomi. This will give you some idea of the complicated flavor of these negotiations.

Now it is time to return to Pokagon's wigwam and visit with Elizabeth and the old Shaman of the Tonquish.

As they sit together by the campfire, night after night, their thoughts go back to the old days when Tonquish was alive, and Sawak, and Skash, and Nawme, and Ninewa. All gone now.

Even young and handsome Tongah or Telonga, as some called him, murdered in a savage brawl. They were glad that Mrs. Tongah, his widow, was with them, and her daughter who had named her child Acuarie in memory of Sawak's sister and Pokagon's first wife. They were among the leaders of the clan and they held their ground with pride and dignity.

The government knew their power and acknowledged it when they granted Mrs. Tongah two sections of land after Tongah's death, the only Potowatomi woman, in the Kappler Treaty Book, so honored.

The old Shaman spoke of happier days on Plymouth Mound when he had presided at the installation of Tongah. As the fire dimmed down the group separated for the night.

11. Chicago Treaty of 1833 Follows Jackson's Guidelines

"Shall not one line lament our forest race,
Struck out for you from wild creation's face?
Freedom—the selfsame freedom you adore—
Bade us defend our violated shore."
— Simon Pokagon, Potowatomi

Since the beginning of our American dream one of the basic safeguards has been the assurance that our constitutional rights as free citizens will be respected.

To help assure this protection our 'Founding Fathers' in their wisdom devised a system of checks and balances, and created an institution we call the Supreme Court. This system gives some stability to the difficult art of democratic self-government. From time to time we have floundered in the valley of dissent and conflict, of Civil War, of financial crisis, of turmoil and struggle here and abroad.

Yet, in spite of these enormous difficulties, our peacetime pursuit of life, liberty, and happiness has continued. The majority of our citizens believe in our system. We have fought and we may fight again to defend our freedom. To us these United States is truly our home, our land of liberty and of hope and opportunity. This is our country. God Bless America.

71

But to Chief Simon Pokagon, Potowatomi, friend of the Tonquish, son of Chief Leopold Pokagon, grandson of the great Chief Topenebee, freedom was not just a white man's word. His Indian soul knew freedom too. When he wrote the lines quoted above he is telling us something. Maybe we should listen.

Today, true freedom is challenged everywhere, he said. Is freedom just for us or for all mankind regardless of race, color, or creed? Let us think about this if we would preserve our own liberty. This world of the atom bomb can not survive half slave and half free. Let us mean it when we say, 'Let there be peace on earth.'

We return to the treaty room. Who is this old chief coming toward us in a headpiece of full eagle feathers, he wondered. Doesn't he know that you do not wear eagle feathers at a peace meeting? Doesn't he own a head dress? Oh, its old Weesaw! We have been through a lot together. He's a decent sort. He means well and he's still as handsome as the devil. But he has more words than wisdom. I must guard my tongue or sixteen different versions of the treaty will be babbled all over the camp before morning.

But Weesaw is a fine shot with the hunting bow. I remember how he kept us all from starving one winter. Now there are only about 150 in his little band and we have twice that many, Pokagon thought. Weesaw lives over in Newton's woods at Little Prairie Ronde in Volinia Township, Cass County.

"Oh Lord, spare us now!," Pokagon exclaimed and because he was a good Catholic I knew he meant what he said. "There is old Shavehead trying to avoid me as usual. He's as ugly as sin and twice as dangerous. I wish he had stayed home. He'll make big trouble before this day is out, I imagine."

But a strangely subdued Shavehead was standing quietly talking to his aide who seemed awed by his surroundings. Shavehead's band had dwindled to about seventy and their camp was near Shavehead Lake in Porter Township, Cass County.

Pokagon whispered to me, "Let me tell you what he tried to get away with just last week. Why, the man's insane! He tipped over a poor, settler's wagon dumping the man, his wife and three children into the river. They saved themselves by hanging onto the wagon. Old Shavehead wouldn't help them until they paid him a large toll! After he collected, he let them go. Now he is armed to the teeth and he has set up his own toll booth down by the river and proposes to tax every white settler who comes along. The man's crazy! They'll lock him up for sure, or somebody will pick him off. Look at him! He's almost sober for a change. What a disgrace! It's an embarrassment. But I can't do anything. They are kin of ours."

"Now we must turn our thoughts away from small matters and face the political realities of our pathetic situation," Pokagon continued. "I have learned a lot about that man in the White House in the weeks I have been here waiting for them all to arrive. And let me tell you, my friend, our situation is hopeless. But I hope to be able to save a little land for us and Tonquish out of this holocaust." I saw tears in his eyes as he walked away, and I also was disheartened by his evaluation of the real situation. How much did Leopold Pokagon really know?

Did he know that "Old Hickory," Andrew Jackson, seventh President of these United States, wanted to go home to the Hermitage near Nashville for a good, long rest?

The Indian problem was just one more sweat and not the top priority item on Jackson's agenda. After the acrimonious, Webster-Hayne debate, and the eternal oratory of Henry Clay, Daniel Webster, and John C. Calhoun, Jackson decided that he had earned a rest. Old Hickory was glad and grateful that he had the Hermitage to retreat to.

And he was thankful that he had spoken up for the Constitution at that stupid Jefferson Day Dinner. The whole country had eventually applauded his speech. It was a great rallying cry, "The Union Must Be Preserved." That certainly took the wind out of Hayne's sails. Hayne thought all he had to do was rave on and on about Jefferson and that nobody there would stop him.

According to Martin Van Buren, the Vice President, who had accompanied President Jackson to the Jefferson Dinner, Jackson wrote his speech on a piece of scrap paper while he was waiting for an opportunity to deliver it. He was not on the program and he could barely endure listening to "all that claptrap" about state's rights. "I think I saved the country," he was to exclaim later over this most dramatic incident. And, indeed, Jackson's remarkably moving speech was to be the bulwark of those forces who defended the Constitution for the next thirty years.

But Jackson's money policies had gotten the country into serious difficulties. To make matters worse, the United States Treasury building was totally destroyed by a mysterious fire. The valuables were somehow saved but many records were lost.

An audit showed that the Congress had given away to the new states about eight million acres of land. But the government seemed to be going broke. Jackson was having serious trouble with the banks, and so he ordered his Secretary of the Treasury to withdraw some money and give it over to certain preferred banks. The first Secretary of the Treasury

74

refused to obey so Jackson appointed another one and up-ped the amount. Duane, the new Treasurer, withdrew about 10 million dollars, a horrendous sum for that time, and loaned it to the preferred banks.

The entire country was in a state of near panic over this. Some thought "Old Hickory" should be impeached. But he held his course, not influenced by the clamoring public, and in due time his ship righted itself. The banks loaned the money freely, and credit and confidence returned. The value of the dollar was gradually restored.

This was the state of affairs when the poor Powatomi and the other Algonquin in the woods of Chicago were dream-ing of treaty money. When Pokagon walked to the treaty table he faced that wily, old Indian fighter, Zachary Taylor.

And Taylor paused a long, long time before he spoke. The two leaders faced each other, eye to eye, and neither gave an inch.

The next morning came and once again we walk with Chief Leopold Pokagon past that battered stockade gate and the entrance palisade and on to the inner bastion of this patched-up piece of old logs they call Fort Dearborn. Once it was almost burned to the ground. (*Remnants of the fire are still visible on the east portico. But they have done a good job of putting it together again with solid hand-pegged logs and gobs of tough, porous clay. The shake roof looks fairly new.*) Pokagon seems very pensive. Is he remembering the time in 1812 when he joined Topenebee in trying to save the whites from the massacre near here? That was more than twenty years ago. He had saved about a dozen. Will they remember? Will they temper their so-called justice with mercy?

Let's go into the Treaty Room. That's the main, large room in the heart of the Fort. Look at those flags and that beautiful table! These Chemokomen (Americans with long knives) certainly know how to dress up this old place. And look at those beautiful feathers on the quill pens. Gorgeous!

They are ready for us, Pokagon thought, and they will expect me to touch that pen before this day is over. I'll not sign until I strike a hard bargain. I'll take the Tonquish Shaman's advice about saving the land. It's our last chance to hold some ground in this territory, and he promised himself that he would serve the Shaman and the Tonquish cause as well as his own by holding out for a private reservation by the old lake in Michigan. If I give them so much, they should give me a little.

Pokagon looked around the room to see who was there. He wanted to find Mrs.Tongah to protect her from the rabble. She was in charge of the Tonquish since Tongah's death. The government had given her half a section of land near Mendon at Nottowa Sipe in St. Joseph County. The only Indian woman in the world to be so respected by a white man's government. She had warned Pokagon about watching their eyes. "You can always tell a liar by his eyes," she said. He was glad that Mrs. Tongah had not come into this rough crowd, and that his Elizabeth had probably persuaded her to stay by their own campfire at the Pokagon wigwam in the woods near the lake.

Chief Pokagon was making daily pilgrimages to Fort Dearborn to try to negotiate a fair settlement for the Potowatomi-Chippewa-Ottawa interests he represented. But secretly the wise old chief knew he was doomed before he had begun. He was, however, very determined to salvage something from the wreckage. Now it is September 1833 and there isn't much time left.

Pokagon was born in 1775 of a Chippewa father and an

Ottowa mother. His wife, Elizabeth, was a Potowatomi. Early in life Pokagon had been adopted by the great chief Topinabe. Like the late lamented Chief Tonquish, who also was of mixed blood, Pokagon always knew where his best interests lay. Although a good man, he also was basically a politician who had forged to the front in the control and direction of the tribes.

On this day, Sept. 26, 1833, he was standing in the crowded, overheated main room at Fort Dearborn, face to face with a wily Indian-fighter and a stubborn, dangerous adversary, Col. Zachary Taylor. Fresh from a triumph over Black Hawk, Taylor was in no mood for compromise.

"Now Pokagon," the sharp voice of the colonel pierced the air like a razor's edge, "You must remember the tide. It does not move backward at the bidding of any Indian."

"The tide, Pokagon, favors the white man. And you know that. And you know that I cannot change it. Neither can you. Can you command the wind? Can you move the sun? Neither can you move this horde of white settlers who would own this land. They will take it from you and neither you nor I can stop them.

"If you are smart, and I think you are, you will head for a safe port. Trim your sails, man. I make you no promise I cannot deliver. And I promise you a large, beautiful land across the Mississippi in Kansas. Take your people to Kansas. The tide has turned, Pokagon. You can NOT stay here. If you do not accept what I would give you now, you will lose it all. Do you understand? LOSE IT ALL!" he repeated emphatically, pounding on the table.

"I understand this," Pokagon announced in excellent English without a trace of dialect, clear cut, precise, confident. "And I understand perfectly what you are about to do, but I think you have forgotten something. And it is something very important to yourself and to your people. You must consider it or the tide will turn against you, too."

"And what the hell is that?" was Taylor's impatient response. Perhaps he was addressing the chief, but probably he was startled by a near riot which suddenly had erupted in the back of the room.

A half dozen militia men with bayonets bared quickly appeared on the scene and escorted the rioters from the area.

The instigator was tipsy, old Chief Shavehead who was to spend some time in Fort Dearborn's brig. Shavehead, you may recall, had named himself chief tollgate keeper on the river near his home base in Porter Township, Cass County. He had a lucrative "business" holding up passing settlers, charging an outrageous toll for permission to ford "my river."

The room quieted down and Chief Pokagon and Col. Taylor were about to resume their discussion when suddenly another interruption occurred.

A breathless messenger rushed in with a letter for Taylor. After a hasty glance, he explained:

"Bad news, Pokagon, I must leave for Washington at once. I leave you in good hands. Listen to my advice. Go to Kansas. My commissioners will spell it out for you. Listen to them."

Before the day was over Pokagon had signed the treaty but as he took up the goose quill pen to make his mark the tears began to fall on his old buckskin jacket. He bravely faced the Chemokemon officers who had come to watch the proceeding and, speaking directly to the government agents, he said in a strong, clear voice, "I would rather die

78

than do this. But it is better to endure a wrong than to commit one."

Love thy neighbor," the black robes had taught him well. This was a good man who every night of life said, *"Nossimaw wawking, kithiwa kiaik anosowin.* This is our Father, Who art in Heaven." His later life attests that he truly believed in the Christian faith.

With a stroke of the pen Pokagon had forfeited more than six million acres in northern Illinois, southern Michigan and parts of Wisconsin and northern Ohio.

It was the end of dominance for the "Three Fires" in the Middle West. Although he could write English well, Pokagon refused to make more than a half-hearted mark with the goose quilled pen, but it was enough to open the floodgates of the white settlers.

The treaty of Oct. 27 ceded the reservation at Pokagon's village of the Tonquish band. Pokagon was given $2,000 in cash and his wife, Elizabeth, was given two whole sections. Mrs. Tongah, who had control of Tongah's land, was given an additional half-section. So these people salvaged a little out of the pillage.

In this Byzantine world of broken promises and bartered land, it is not surprising to discover that only one of these so-called "Reservations" was in Indian hands five years later.

12. Treaty of 1833

There were a number of other chiefs and head men who signed the treaties of 1833 with Pokagon. The document bore the signatures of the three Indian Commissioners who signed on the part of the United States. They were George B. Porter, Thomas J. V. Owen and William Weatherford. All of the Indians made their mark, or "touched the pen." The list for September 27 reads as follows:

G. B. Porter,	Maatch-kee,
Th. J. V. Owen,	Kaw-bai-me-sai,
William Weatherford,	Wees-ke-qua-tap,
To-pen-e-bee,	Ship-she-wuh-no,
We-saw,	Wah-co-mah-o-pe-tuk,
Ne-kaw-nosh-kee,	Ne-so-wah-quet,
Wai-saw-o-ko-ne-aw,	Shay-o-no,
Po-ka-gon,	Ash-o-nees,
Kai-kaw-tai-mon,	Mix-i-nee,
Pe-pe-ah,	Ne-wah-ox-sec,
Ne-see-waw-bee-tuck,	Sauk-e-mau,
Kitchee-bau,	Shaw-waw-nuk-wuk-,
Pee-chee-ko,	Mo-rah,
Nai-gaw-geucke,	Suk-see,
Wag-maw-kan-so,	Quesh-a-wase,
Mai-go-sai,	Pat-e-go-to,
Nai-chee-wai,	Mash-ke-oh-see,
Aks-puck-sick,	Mo-nase,
Kaw-kai-mai,	Wab-e-kaie,

Mans-kai-sick,
Pam-ko-wuck,
No-taw-gai
Kauk-muck-kisin,
Wee-see-mon,
Mo-so-ben-net
Kee-o-kum,

Shay-oh-new,
Mo-gua-go,
Pe-qua-shuc,
A-muwa-noc-sey,
Kau-ke-che-ke-to,
Shaw-waw-nuk-wuk,

In presence of

Wm. Lee. D. Ewing,
  Secretary to the
  commission,
E. A. Brush,
Luther Rice, interpreter,
James Conner, interpreter,
Joseph Bertrand, jr.,
  interpreter,
Geo. Kercheval,
  sub Indian agent,
B. B. Kercheval,
Thomas Forsyth,
Daniel Jackson,
  of New York
J. E. Schwarz,
  adjutant-general M. M.
Robt. A. Kinzie,
G. S. Hubbard,
Geo. Bender, major
  Fifth Regiment Infantry
D. Wilcox, captain Fifth
  Regiment,
J.M. Baxley, captain
  Fifth Infantry,
R. A. Forsyth, U.S. Army,

J. L. Thompson,
  lieutenant
  Fifth Infantry,
J. Allen, lieutenant Fifth
  Infantry
P. Maxwell, assistant surgeon
U.S.
  Army,
Geo. F. Turner, assistant
  surgeon U. S. Army,
L. M. Taylor,
Pierre Menard, fils,
Jacob Beeson,
Samuel Humes Porter,
Edmd, Roberts,
Jno. H. Kinzie,
Jas. W. Berry,
Gabriel Godfroy, jr.
Geo. Hunt,
A. H. Arndt,
Andw. Porter,
Isaac Nash,
Richard J. Hamilton.

L. T. Jamison, lieutenant
 U.S. Army,
O. K. Smith, lieutenant
 Fifth Infantry

———

SCHEDULE "A"

Referred to in the Article supplementary to the Treaty, containing the sums payable to Individuals, in lieu of Reservations of Land.

	Dollars.
Po-ka-gon	2000
Rebecca Burnett[*]	500
Mary Burnett[*]	250
Martha Burnett (R. A. Forsyth Trustee)	250
Madeline Bertrand	200
Joseph Bertrand Junr	200
Luke Bertrand Junr	200
Benjamin Bertrand	200
Lawrence Bertrand	200
Theresa Bertrand	200
Amable Bertrand	200
Julianne Bertrand	200
Joseph H. Bertrand	100
Mary M. Bertrand	100
M. L. Bertrand	100
John B. Du Charme	200
Elizabeth Du Charme (R. A. Forsyth Trustee)	800
George Henderson	400
Mary Nado and children	400
John Bt. Chandonai[†]	1000

Charles Chandonai[†]	400
Mary Chandonai	400
Mary St. Comb and children	300
Sa-gen-nais' daughter	200
Me-chain, daughter of Pe-che-co	200
Alexis Rolan	200
Polly Neighbush	200
Francois Page's wife and children	200
Pierre F. Navarre's children	100
Jarmont (half breed)	100
Ten thousand dollars	$10,000

[*]}Edward Brooks Trustee for each{
[†]}For each of whom R. A. Forsyth is Trustee{

———

Sept. 27, 1833.

Agreeably to the stipulations contained in the Articles supplementary to the Treaty, there have been purchased and delivered at the request of the Indians, Goods, Provisions, and Horses to the amount of fifteen thousand dollars (leaving the balance to be supplied hereafter ten thousand dollars.)

As evidence of the purchase and delivery as aforesaid, under the direction of the said commissioners, and that the whole of the same been received by the said Indians, and the said George B. Porter, Thomas J. V. Owen, and William Weatherford, and the undersigned chiefs and head men on behalf of the said United Nation of Indians, have hereunto set their hands the twenty-seventh day of September, in the year of our Lord one thousand eight hundred and thirty-three.

G. B. Porter,	To-pen-e-bee,
Th. J. V. Owen,	Wee-saw,
William Weatherford,	Ne-kaw-nosh-kee,
	Po-ka-gon.

In the 1832 "Treaty with the Potowatomi" Mrs. Togah is mentioned as follows:

To Togah, a Potowatomie woman, one quarter section:

To Mary Ann Bruner, one quarter section.

What is the relationship, if any between Mrs. Togah and Mary Ann Bruner? Where are the present day heirs of Togah? What became of this land? Your author has not presently found answers to these questions.

13. Many Changes Mark History of Tonquish Plain Area

Yesterday, as I walked along Tonquish Creek on the way home, I thought of the many changes that had taken place along this babbling brook. I remembered the removals, the transitions of time and place, and I mourned the losses that seem to accompany the aging process for brooks and people.

I remember when Penniman Avenue was a gravel road, and when I could take the "Interurban" down town, and shop at Hudsons and Himmelhoch's, Healy's and Tuttle & Clark. I remember when it was fun to have luncheon at the Statler Hotel. And I remember when the top of that hill that I am staring at now was crowned by the lovely Walter Kellogg Sumner home. I remember. I remember. But what does this have to do with change and the Indian, and early Detroit? Quite a bit! Wait and see. It will come to you too, if you live long enough!

Some of the Walter Kellogg Sumner papers are in the Burton Collection of the Detroit Public Library, and in an address Mr. Sumner made years ago to the Plymouth Historical Society he mentioned the fact that his grandfather Kellogg told him that he remembered the time when a remnant of the Tonquish clan camped across the street from the

Sumner home. The lovely Christian Science Church crowns that hill today.

Charles C. Royce's monumental book, "Indian Land Cessions in the United States," has something to say about change and Chief Tonquish. With reference to the Treaty of 1827, Royce quotes a government edict which states, "In order to consolidate some of the dispersed bands of the Potowatomi tribe in the Territory of Michigan at a point removed from the road leading from Detroit to Chicago and as far as practicable from the settlements of the whites, it is agreed that the following track of land heretofore reserved for the use of said tribe shall be ceded to the United States."

Further reading in Royce reveals that this reference is to the Tonquish village on Eight Mile Road between the Nine and 10 Mile posts on the north branch of the Rouge River and extending south into the Livonia-Westland area.

The Tonquish were being pushed out toward Plymouth and then westward. At this time some of them joined friends in the Nottawa Sipe Reservation south of Mendon. Others joined the Pokagons. Some retreated to Walpole Island, and some went north into the Alpena area and into Wisconsin and Northern Michigan.

I remember that among the Julia Gatlin Moore Papers at the Burton Library is a reference to some of the last survivors of these Indians.

In the spring of 1927, according to Moore, a large group of them celebrated the centennial of their removal in solemn rites at a branch of the Rouge adjacent to Ford Field, Dearborn. It is known that these Indians came into the Plymouth area at that time and removed something pertinent to their celebration. Perhaps they dug up the old black altar and took it with them. Extensive investigation reveals nothing except that they probably were here and they were digging for something.

The Indians from the Alpena area made their journey to the Rouge in the old style. According to Julia Moore, they ignored villages, signs, cities, highway markers and other developments of modern civilization and did their best to try to follow the trail their forefathers had followed 100 years before. They brought their wigwams, totem poles, and other equipment in the same manner as their ancesters.

Everyone was surprised to see them. There was no trouble and no conflict with the authorities. After the ceremony was over they swarmed into the city, watched a baseball game between Dearborn and Fordson, applauded the victors enthusiastically, and then silently departed the way they came. They never have been seen in the area since. (Any information any reader can give me as to where these Indians are now, and what became of the black ceremonial altar, will be deeply appreciated. We would very much like to exhibit this altar at the Plymouth Historical Society.)

According to Charles Royce, "The legal fiction of recognizing the tribes as independent nations with which the United States could enter into solemn treaty, after it had continued nearly a hundred years, was finally done away with."

The effect was to bring under direct control of Congress all transactions with the Indians. As of March 3, 1871, the Indians' title to lands in the public domain virtually had been extinguished. This was the end of an era.

It was as if all treaties ever signed merely had been temporary, political expedients, and that the Indian was totally dependent on the bounty of Congress. This was the way it was for the poor Indian. It created a fundamental change in his own definition of what he could and could not do. He felt he had lost his freedom, but he had not lost his spirit.

Today we are seeing a resurgence of the old Indian spirit of independence, and a desire to get back some of the land that was once theirs.

And what about the white people? There were traumatic changes for them, too. The poor settler along the Tonquish, and everywhere else, often came with only a few dollars, some tools, a poor, struggling family, and the shirt on his back. He had to carve a home out of the wilderness. Traumatic change was an intimate part of his life. He lived with it every day. The vicissitudes of life were very real to him.

Change seems to be inherent in all life.

This is the way it was for the Indian, and this is the way for us today.

"America, the beautiful" has seen at least five different owners in 500 years. Here is a kind of kaleidoscope of history which will give us a condensed version of these changes.

When Tonquish Creek was young, the Hopewell Indians were building mounds near Plymouth. They were artists of a high order and their culture survived for a thousand years. Today, remnants of their mounds are strung all over southern Michigan. But where are the people who built them? No one knows.

Then let us remember the Vikings who came to this land at an early date.

The changing picture moves on and we pause at 1492. Columbus and Spain claimed ownership of this area then, and at a somewhat later date, Spain raised its flag over an outpost in the St. Joseph Valley. The treasures of the Inca, the Aztecs, and the Hopewells went back to Spain in golden bundles. Where are they now?

In 1497 Tonquish Creek belonged to Great Britain. And

with the defeat of the Spanish Armada in 1588, England had more ships with which to pursue her claim to sovereignty. She claimed this land—all of it.

1609 found King Charles of England calling this country a part of his new territory of Virginia. Then in 1629 it was chartered to Massachusetts. By 1656 Tonquish Plain was a kind of province of the Dominion of New England. The Indians who lived here never would believe that!

Time rolls on and change is inevitable. About the year 1700 this whole area belonged to New France and the ribbon farms of the French bordered the Detroit River as far as the eye could see. For the next seventy-five years ownership see-sawed between France and Great Britain.

When the American Revolution finally ended with the Treaty of Paris in 1783, there was a tremendous change in all of these United States. And we have been celebrating this on the Fourth of July ever since.

The Tonquish Plain area belonged to the great Northwest Territory in 1787. Then came the French Revolution. It began about 1789 and ended with the coup d'etat of Napoleon in 1799. It had great influence upon our country and changed many of our folkways, attitudes and customs.

By 1800 this area where we now live officially was designated "Indian Territory" on most of the maps of that time. In 1805 we became a part of the Michigan Territory and remained part of the Michigan Territory throughout all of the Indian Treaty changes of that period. Finally Michigan complied with certain conditions imposed upon her, was admitted to the union of the United States. This was a cause for celebration.

But by 1846 we were at war again. Our attempt to acquire Texas led to the Mexican War, a skirmish which was settled by the Treaty of Gaudaloupe-Hidalgo in 1848.

Less than fifteen years later, on January 9, 1861, to be

89

exact, a cannon's roar off Fort Sumpter, S.C., signaled the beginning of one of the most horrible conflicts in our history—the Civil War or, as southerners insisted on calling it, "the War Between the States."

Let us retreat to the old log church in the wild wood where we left the remnants of the Tonquish and listen to the sweet voice of Acuarie who is singing softly to the beautiful boy baby in her arms as they walk toward the little log church nearby.

> The Voice of the Turtle
> is heard in our land
> In the spring of the year
> When the broom corn stand
> Grows green in the sun
> Near the sea and the shore
> As the world turns 'round
> And the buds break free
> Coming forth from the ground
> Listen, as the turtle's sound
> Whispers o'er the ancient land
> Of change. Of time unending.
> While the golden globe
> Turns 'round and 'round
> And around again

Acuarie was trying to remember the ancient "Song of the Turtle"—the muhsheegeh of chasgied—that her Chippewa grandmother had often sung to her. Although she was living among the protective, hospitable Potowatomi, Acuarie sometimes longed for the voices of her childhood. They always would be dear to her.

Mrs. Tongah, Acuarie's Potowatomi mother-in-law, was glad to have found shelter with her cousin (Elizabeth Pokagon) since her husband, Tongah, had been killed in a savage brawl near the ancient mound at Grand Rapids.

Tongah was the successor to old Chief Tonquish who had been shot to death by Captain William Macomb and some irate settlers. This slaughter took place on Tonquish Plain near Plymouth, Mich., in 1819. The boy baby in Acuarie's arms was little Toga—only grandson of Chief Tonquish, he was also known to his contemporaries as Toga.

Holding little Toga close to her heart and leading the six-year-old Elizabeth, her other child, and Mrs. Tongah, the little group joined the throng streaming into the church at Chichipe Outipe Sipe.

What is a Tonquish grandson doing here in the arms of a Chippewa mother, being carried into a Catholic chapel to hear a priest from Rennes, France, address them in broken English and pidgin Potowatomi about the latest garbled government edict? How did they wander so far from their comfortable old home on Tonquish Plain? What strange fate has brought them to this pass?

Pictured opposite:

The Wolf River, Kansas. A 19th century picture painted by Albert Bierstadt. Reproduced here by courtesy of The Founders Society of the Detroit Institute of Arts
The Bierstadt masterpiece was a Founders Society Purchase through the Dexter M. Ferry, Jr. Fund.

14. Pokagon's Tonquish Clan Near "Trail of Tears"

After Black Hawk's final defeat August 27, 1832, tremendous winds of change nearly blew the country apart.

From Texas to Missouri, from the Everglades of Florida to the hills of Tennessee, from Kentucky's ridges to the lakes of Michigan, the Indian was being pushed toward the West.

The white settler—the "Long Knives" or "chemokomen" as the Indians called them—had taken over after the Chicago Treaty of 1833. A few remnants of the Pokagons and the Tonquish clung to their homes in the St. Joseph Valley, but even these poor hovels were being invaded by the settlers.

Meanwhile, in the South, vast armies of Indians were being forcibly removed. Most the Cherokees, the Creeks, the Chickasaws, the Shawnees, the Seminoles, the Chocktaws, the Senecas, the Delawares, and thousands more were learning about broken promises and meaningless treaties as they were marched into alien lands. There many would perish from cold, hunger, white man's liquor, and diseases. These removals were the first step in the deliberate destruction of a whole mass of people.

(I am grateful that space limitations do not permit me to dwell on this ghastly story in gory detail. Many volumes have been written about the pitiful plight of the Indian. My particular interest has been that group of Plymouth Tonquish who left this area about 1827, eight years after Chief Tonquish was killed. Some of them went north to the Cross Village where they tried to establish themselves among the Ottowas. They did not receive a very warm reception. Others went to Grayling and to Alpena. Some retreated to Walpole Island and tried to live among the Chippewas. Others just hid out in the forests. They formed independent enclaves within the white boundaries, and a few live in this manner today. A few intermarried with blacks to create another breed of people; while others married white citizens. Many people of Indian descent live as white people today. While they feel they have gained security, they have lost a marvelous mystical heritage.)

The Indians of our story went to Notoawa Sipe south of Mendon in St. Joseph County.

Their leaders were in touch with Chief Leopold Pokagon who lived in adjacent Cass County. Our Tonquish were not far from their cousins, the Topash clan who lived near Buchanan. So we prescribe limits to our story for the reasons stated.

Going back in time we create an imaginary interview.

We return to our walk with Acuarie and Little Toga. Mrs. Tongah and young Elizabeth. We are headed for a special meeting that the authorities have forced Father Petit to call at his church at Chichipe Outipe. What a beautiful morning, but I fear for my friends and for what this day may bring forth.

My questioning has been persistent and we have walked for miles so we are tired. Suddenly Acuarie broke her silence to reveal to me some of her private thoughts.

"Helena, I will try once more to answer your questions. You keep beating the drum. Why? Are you writing a book? What do you really want to know?"

Overjoyed at this response after a long silence, I said, "Tell me about your genealogy. Who was Tonquish?"

"That's a difficult question," she replied, "but I'll try to tell you. We do not count people the way you probably do. Among our people a chief may have several wives. But in our family the record is clear, I think.

"I don't know everything but I'll tell you what I do know. It is not in print but is handed down from generation to generation, like your Bible, maybe. My mother, Tongah's wife, was a daughter of your Plymouth Tonquish, and she is a sister of Elizabeth Pokagon who is Chief Pokagon's second wife.

"I was named for her, Acuarie, an old Indian name. She was my grandmother's cousin. That Acuarie was the daughter of Chief Sawak who was a brother of Topenebe, the supreme chief of all the Potowatomi for nearly forty years. Topenebe had a sister who was very beautiful. She was called Princess Kaukema, and he had another brother, Chief Chebass. They were all children of the great chief of Indiana and Illinois. His headquarters were at Niles.

"Tonquish was a very minor chief—not a big shot like Menominee or Pokagon. The truth is we do not know where he came from. Some said he was a Chippewa. He was an old man when he married my grandmother. She was a Chippewa, but he could speak Potowatomi fluently. It's a different dialect but has the same roots.

"We are all Ojibwa from the Algonquin. Tonquish drank too much sometimes. But he was smart and brave. Everybody liked him so they made him chief. It was sad how he lost his son, young Toga. They shot him, you know. My son is Toga, grandson of your Tonquish. I will never take my son to Kansas. Never!" And those deep brown eyes became twin pools of determination and tears as she vowed to protect her family and her home in Michigan.

We must hurry. The Pokagons are waiting for us at the church. Did you know that Leopold owns that land in Silver Creek? He bought it with the Chicago Treaty money. They can't take it from him. It's registered in your court. We may go there."

"We are hungry. There is not enough game left. Nothing left here. They have taken our hunting grounds, and our men spend their treaty money for liquor. Only Pokagon stays sober. He is smart. We starve. I do not have enough money for food and I have no milk for my baby.

"Father Petit tries, poor man. Our old gods must have died. They have deserted us. Now we must listen to a white priest, speaking Latin in old fashioned Potowatomi with a French accent. It's pathetic, really."

By now we had reached the Pokagons at the church door.

Affectionate greetings were exchanged and we proceeded to seats which had been reserved for us up in the front. The church was packed with about 300 and a few white traders and government officials.

As the bell tolled old Chief Menominee stepped forward to try to comfort them. He spoke in the compassionate tones of a father speaking to his children. Father Petit is ill, he said, and regretted that he could not be with them today. Menominee said that his trip to Washington had been successful and that they were assured of the best land in Kansas.

The truth was somewhat different as Menominee well knew. As a matter of fact the old records show that when Menominee personally protested the removal to Kansas to President Martin VanBuren, Old Kinderhook, in his aloof and haughty way stated: "I do not wish to speak of it," and walked away. Then the old chief visited the war office where he spoke with the secretary and was bluntly told, "Menominee, your lands are lost."

Determined to make the way easier for his Potowatomi if

he could, Menominee pledged to them that he would go with them to Kansas. Then, in a somewhat faltering voice, the old chief said, "That time we have not sought has finally come." Everyone knew what he meant.

Fearing that Menominee would not be effective, one Lewis Sands, an egotistical, pipsqueak of a man and the government's choice for Indian Commissioner, pushed forward and usurped Menominee's place.

In brutally forthright terms the angry Sands said, "That time is now and you must move at once." He added that he had hired ten people to assist them and many large wagons and drivers. The militia would accompany them part of the way, he added. "There is no alternative. You must go now. Today!"

Something in the man's tone stirred the infant, Toga, to a wild and stormy protest. His lusty howls shook the firmament and Acuarie could not comfort him. Chief Pokagon seized upon the racket as a pretext for a hurried departure. Gathering Toga in his arms Pokagon led Acuarie, Elizabeth, and Mrs. Pokagon toward the door. About a dozen faithful friends joined their exodus which was accompanied the whole time by Toga's unrelenting howls. It was as though the old Toga (grandfather Tonquish) once again had driven his knife into the good earth, protesting "No, No, No!"

The little group was surprised at the outer door by several armed, bayonetted militiamen who barrd their way. Through the window Pokagon caught his first glimpse of an army of militia who had completely surrounded the church while Menominee had spoken. In the distance he saw the flames of the village going up in smoke.

15. Tragic Trip to Kansas Brings Death to Many

Chief Pokagon was startled by the young militiaman's hard face and the sharp look of the bayonet which barred his exit at the church door.

Still holding the howling Tonquish baby, little Toga, in his arms, Pokagon stepped back into the rear of the church and signaled Menominee with a special hand sign which alerted him to the danger outside. Then in a calm, assured voice, Pokagon addressed the Indian Commisioner, Lewis Sands, "We have our own wagons. They are waiting for us. Let my people go."

Then Menominee hurried over to Sands and was heard to say, "This man is Pokagon and he has a right to his land. Let him go, or you will hear from all of us again."

Surprised by this move and the evident mass support by a majority of the crowd, Sands paused and angrily turned toward Pokagon. He made a move as if to strike him, then paused again and pushed his way past the chief, yelled at the guard, "Get them out of here. Go Pokagon and don't you ever come back here again."

Acuarie grabbed young Toga and made a dash for the door, but Leopold grasped her arm and whispered, "Slow down, girl. Show them no fear. Walk slowly. Wait for your mother."

With a sudden, clear perception of his message, Acquarie stopped in her tracks and waited for the others. She tested her charms by smiling at the armed guard who had never left her side, and she was delighted when he returned her smile. When they reached the wagon he assisted her to climb in and, at her direction, helped all the others. They drove off rather slowly.

Although surrounded by an army of some 200 armed troops, not one shot was fired. Pokagon's old horse, the same one that had carried him and Johnny Appleseed along the old trail south some years before, was ready to gallop home, and the chief had some difficulty in holding him to a more moderate pace. He wanted to go slowly so that the rest of his group could keep up with the procession. Elizabeth said, "We're going home, Leopold. I'm so glad. It's been a very, long day."

They were headed for Bertrand and Pokagon's old village near the Indiana border. Anticipating the present troubles Leopold had purchased land in 1837 some miles north of there in Cass County at Silver Creek. The Chicago Treaty of Sept. 26, 1833 had forced him to rethink his interests in Michigan property.

A supplement to the Chicago Treaty had given him outright ownership of certain lands in Cass County. And now he had to decide where he wanted to live and what would be the best for his band of 300. The treaty had forced most of the "Woods Potowatomi" to give up all claims to tribal reservations along the St. Joseph River. Nottawa Sippi was closed to them too. The Tonquish had gone to Walpole Island, or back into Canada, or north to Alpena. A few went to Kansas, and a few remained with Pokagon. Only old Shavehead was allowed to stay in Porter Township. He was so mean no one really cared. His band had dwindled to about seventy-five and the government was tired of fighting with him. They were waiting for him to die.

According to the Cass County history, Leopold Pokagon was the largest taxpayer in the county.

He was assessed some $2,602 as early as 1838. The next highest taxpayer was a white farmer, a wealthy Quaker, who paid $1,690. The Pokagon holdings included 214 acres in Section 14 directly south of the present Catholic Church, 160 acres in Section 21, and another 160 in Section 22. They lived there with a remnant of the Tonquish and called it home. They protected it, paid their taxes, and were good citizens in the community.

Leopold Pokagon died at Silver Creek on July 8, 1841. He was only sixty-six but he was tired and worn by the trials of this life. He had been a good leader to his people, a faithful father, and loyal friend. The entire tribe mourned his death. He was succeeded by his sons, all children of his marriage to Elizabeth, Mrs. Tongah's relative.

Not all of his sons inherited the father's abilities and the eldest one, Paul, was blamed for the split in the settlement after his father's death. Paul was succeeded by his brother, Francis, who was well liked but not too influential. He died in 1877, and then the youngest brother, Simon, became chief. Simon had his father's superior ability and, in addition, had an excellent education at Notre Dame. He authored several books, and wrote articles that appeared in notable magazines of that day including the Review of Reviews and Harpers. He also lectured throughout America.

Leopold Pokagon also left descendants by several daughters of his first wife, Acuarie, a cousin of little Toga's mother, the Acuarie of our story. Leopold's Acuarie was a granddaughter of Anaquiba, the father of Sawak and Topenebe.

At one time these people controlled more than six million acres in Indiana, Illinois, Wisconsin, and southern Michigan. It has been alleged that Topenebee died in July 1826 as a result of a fall from a horse which he had attempted to race while intoxicated. This once brilliant leader may have become an alcoholic. Wilbur Cunningham in his book, "Land of Four Flags," discusses the problem of Topenebee's name appearing on treaties long after his death. One theory is that someone was signing for his son, Topenebee, Jr.

The Reverend Benjamin Petit had been a lawyer in Rennes, France, and had studied for the priesthood in Paris and Vincennes.

Petit had made a promise to his little flock at Chichipe Outipe and he kept his word. He wanted to protect them on the perilous "Trail of Tears" which began on that infamous September day in 1838.

Thanks to little Toga's screams and Pokagon's skill our friends escaped the long march, but we must return to the church to witness what happened there. After the Pokagons escaped others in the crowd of about 200 became very uneasy and some pushed toward the door. To avoid further incidents Sands had a group of militia marched into the outer hall blocking all exits. Then he dismissed the Indians in small groups; each group was accompanied by several armed guards. They were told to go at once to their homes and prepare to leave early the next morning.

One of the saddest events of this gruesome day was the Indian visit to their "village of the dead." They longed to say goodbye to their ancestors. At first, they were silent and in good control of themselves, but then several white people addressed them in a kindly way. Then various Indian chiefs spoke to them and to the dead, explaining what had happened. This was more than they could bear. Such weeping and wailing ensued that the militia became alarmed; so the Indians were forcibly removed.

Morning came and ahead of them loomed a march of more than a thousand miles. Before they left the soldiers fired all the cabins and wigwams. As they marched their eyes smarted with tears and the smoke of the fires that had destroyed their homes.

About 900 were marshaled into a kind of forlorn procession, led by a dragoon carrying the flag of the United States.

Then came the baggage wagons, and then a large wagon carrying the various chiefs including Menominee. When Petit discovered that the chiefs were bound and under guard as "prisoners of war," he moved at once to seek a personal visit with Col. John Tipton, the officer-in-charge.

At Petit's request the chiefs were unbound and were given blankets to sit on and to keep them warm at night.

Next in the procession were the other captives—the women and children mounted on their ponies and most of the men on foot. From the beginning some tried to escape and some succeeded. And many went with the idea of escaping later.

Bringing up the rear in this pitiful caravan were the aged and the sick. They were all lumped together in the jolting wagons, and some were tied like sheep for slaughter. Finally, there came a large wooden cage, a kind of bear trap. It was to be a prison for the unruly and the insane.

There was one physician for the entire caravan and he reported 300 cases of illness in a single day. Many of the ill were helpless children. Imagine the suffering spirit of those who survived. And thank heaven for Petit! They at least had one good friend and comforter along the way.

The route was marked by roadside graves. The food was totally inadequate and often the only drinking water was from stagnant pools. The weather was unusually hot for September and fevers were prevalent.

Petit, true to his word, walked with them all the way and saw them established in their new homes in Kansas. His strength was overtaxed by his devotion, and he died in St. Louis February 10, 1839 on the trip home. Eventually his body was returned and buried under the sanctuary of the chapel of Notre Dame.

Old Chief Menominee, wasted and troubled by the long journey, kept saying, "The President does not know the truth. If he knew . . ." and then his mind would drift away as in a dream. He died enroute to Kansas and they buried him somewhere along the open road. No one ever knew where. But there was a shred of sympathy for him in some circles. Seventy-one years later the sovereign state of Indiana put up a monument for him at Twin Lakes, and Pokagon's granddaughter gave the dedicatory address. It is there today—a reminder of a lost dream.

16. Antoine Cadillac Builds Fort Ponchartrain at d'Etroit

I have chosen to not follow the Indian story to the end along the tragic "Trail of Tears" with all its sadness and horror. I shall return to Detroit to pursue a new and different kind of tale, the story of Antoine Cadillac, the founder of the village on the strait.

Cadillac was the commandant of Fort de Buade near St. Ignace in 1696 when his king, Louis XIV ordered that all the trading posts in the Great Lakes area should be closed. This was a great blow to Cadillac who had been making a lot of money out of the fur trade with the Indians. He was well-liked by the tribes around Michilimackinac. His diplomacy was aided by an ample supply of French brandy of which the Indians were exceedingly fond.

In 1698 Cadillac's adroit and perceptive mind had devised a clever scheme to offset his loss of revenue at de Buade. He decided to go directly to Louis XIV with a plea for a new outpost on the river between Lake. St. Clair and Lake Erie. He knew he could get his Indians to bring their furs from St. Ignace to this new post, and he envisioned a feudal seigniory for himself. He liked the strategic position of a new fort and hoped that Louis would welcome the idea of a strong defense there against the constant threat of encroachment by the British.

Cadillac began at once to pursue his plan through the tenuous French chain of command. He went first to his friend, Governor Frontenac at Quebec, where he was wined and dined and given a wholehearted letter of recommendation. Then he sailed for Paris in October 1698.

After a rugged voyage of several weeks he took a few days off to regain his land legs, buy a new wig and some finery fit for the elegant royal court of the Sun King. His entre was through the minister of the colonies, one Count Pontchartrain, who supported Cadillac's plan.

After some delay, Louis finally made room for the interview in his busy calendar. Louis' life since the revocation of the Edict of Nantes had been one of turmoil and trouble with the Huguenots. And he also was worried about the exchequer which was sadly depleted by his own extravagance and mismanagement. It did not help matters to have all the Protestant forces in Europe threatening war against him.

So Cadillac had the right tack to this elegant wind when he proposed that after the initial expenses were paid by the king, he, Antoine Cadillac, promised to pay all future costs of the Detroit outpost from the fur trade. A large share of the profits would go to Louis. The deal was signed in Paris in 1699.

So Detroit was born in Paris, France, and Louis XIV was its godfather.

June 1701 found Antoine Cadillac in Montreal putting the final touches on his expedition to the proposed place on the straits. Extensive preparations had been made and most of Louis' money was gone. Cadillac was dipping into his own resources to outfit the expedition.

He assembled a small flotilla of twenty-five canoes. On board were fifty coureurs de bois, some of whom had traveled with Cadillac before and knew the area well. And there were fifty well-armed soldiers and 100 Indians. Several canoes were loaded with baubles, beads, and brandy.

Cadillac had his young son, Antoine Jr., age nine, with him. Alphonse de Tonty, brother of LaSalle's loyal aide, Henri deTonty, was second in command. The expedition was accompanied by two priests—a Jesuit, Fr. Francois Vaillant, and a Recollect Father.

The Iroquois were on the warpath again so the little flotilla avoided their country which would have been the short route via the St. Lawrence and Lake Ontario. They paddled the familiar, old fur trader's route along the Ottowa River to Georgian Bay and Lake Huron. Eventually they arrived at a place Cadillac named Fort Ponchartrain d'Etroit. It was a lovely summer's day, July 24, 1701.

17. French Founders Celebrate Building Fort at d'Etroit

Early in the morning of June 5, 1701, after many months of preparation, Antoine Laumet dela Mothe Cadillac and 200 people and goods loaded in twenty-five large canoes swung past the rapids of LaChine near Montreal and headed northwest.

Their goal was to keep the British out of the area the French had long regarded as their private, fur-trader's preserve. They also wanted to block the Iroquois from expansion westward.

In times past they had a small trading post at a place where the river narrows between Lake Erie and Lake Huron. The French had long ago christened it—De Troett or d'Etroit (the strait).

Cadillac had launched his expedition with the financial and moral support of many people including the personal blessing of Louis XIV, King of France; Comte Ponchartrain, minister of the colonies; and Louis de Buade, Comte de Frontenac, the governor of New France.

Probably the 200 souls on board placed more faith in the rugged voyageurs who knew the wilderness route well than they did in their king. These strong voyageurs had no fear of dangers ahead.

But Cadillac, a cautious pragmatist, stationed two well-armed, uniformed soldiers in each canoe. Any skulking coward who would attack would be promptly reprimanded.

Divided up among the 25 canoes with eight people to a boat were about 100 farmers, artisans, and some trusted Algonkin Indians. It was a long, heavily laden flotilla in which Cadillac had packed everything he thought his new colony might need to sustain it for about a month. He trusted to fishing and hunting to supplement their diet.

One canoe was loaded down with beads, baubles and brandy for the thirsty Indians at the trading post. To them French brandy was better than wampum.

There were no women on board. Second in command was Captain de Tonty, and the aides were Lieutenants Dugne and Chacornacle. The first sergeant was a very strong man, a regular Marine, named Jacob Marsac. Cadillac entrusted his lively, nine-year-old- son, Antoine, Jr. to Marsac's care.

Two priests watched out for the spiritual welfare of these hardy souls. One was a Recollect Father, probably Constantin del Halle, the founder of Ste. Anne's, and a Jesuit, Father Francois Valliant de Guerlis.

The expedition head staff was accompanied by two faithful interpreters, the brothers Jean and Francois Faford de Lorme. The de Lormes assisted Father del Halle at Ste. Anne's which is, by the way, the second oldest Catholic church in the United States. The first is at St. Augustine, Fla.

Cadillac would have preferred taking the heavy load the shortest way which would be the St. Lawrence to Lake Ontario and Lake Erie. But he was ordered to go the old route of the fur traders and not disturb the rampaging Iroquois with whom the French were trying to negotiate a treaty.

Many on board never had been outside of the Montreal-Quebec area so they were not displeased with the longer, scenic route. From the Riviere of the Outaouca (Ottowa River), across beautiful Lake Nippissing to the French River there were about thirty portages. By the time they had arrived at the Lake of the Hurons some of the citizens of Montreal were tired of their scenic bargain.

The voyageurs and the Indians paddled energetically down the east side of the lake to the narrow strait and there Cadillac directed them to a cove he knew at a place he called a "Gross Ile."

They built their first camp fire on beautiful Grosse Ile, and settle down for the night. Their morning matins were accompanied by the songs of hundreds of birds and the basso profundo of clear water lapping the stony shore.

For a brief time they thought seriously of building their fort right there. But Cadillac's practical mind rejected the idea. "Not enough forest," he said. "Too hard to defend."

"We need a place where we can see across the river in all directions. We must build a fort with strong bastions for an enfilade. You remember, Tonty, only last year that sandy beach by the narrowest spot of the riviere. That's the best place. Let's explore it again."

So back into the twenty-five canoes, and they paddled the fifteen miles up the river to Cadillac's "meilleur" place. It is a lovely summer's day, July 24, 1701.

They have beached their canoes at a sandy spot near the base of a high cliff which they climb to test the view. Although only about 50 feet high Cadillac pronounced the scene, "Magnifique."

They were delighted to find a parklike, partially cleared place that was almost level. Perhaps it was an old Indian

110

baggatwany field, a game which the Indians played like football. Today it is called LaCrosse.

"Magnifique," Cadillac kept saying as he paced off the dimensions for the fort. Then he ordered, in a most urgent demanding voice, "Attaquer." In other words, pitch in, attack the work. All were as anxious as he to be settled again and so they went to their assigned tasks with true Gallic gusto.

The courer de bois headed for the dense forest which surrounded the place and began to fell the trees for shelter. The soldiers assisted by the Indians brought the supplies to the top of the hill. The artisans and farmers stayed with Cadillac and at his direction built a temporary shelter for the night, and laid the foundations for a warehouse and the little log church of Ste. Anne's.

The air was electric with the sound of falling timber and the chopping and clinking of logs being welded together without the aid of nails or metal clamps of any kind. Before the sun went down they had accomplished their tasks.

First night, they tapped a cask of "eau de vie" and joyously sang together the old boat songs of the voyageurs—"Ala Clair Fontaine," "La Jolie Canadienne," and the rest. Because they were faithful subjects of the king they did not forget to toast "Vive le Roi," and "Vive Le Cadillac" and "Vive le Ponchartrain" until the cask ran dry. Their delightful songs attracted nearby Indians who were able to communicae with other Algonkin in their party. It was a joyous time of camaraderie and happiness. The Indians and the French got along well together. Cadillac made sure of that.

Forty-six days, more than thirty portages and three terrific storms were behind them. And all was well—all had survived. They felt that they had earned a celebration and, indeed, they had. They exclaimed, "Oh, joyous day!" And before the day was over most of them said a prayer of sin-

111

cere gratitude for finding Detroit. It was almost like being home again.

Today this area is in the Civic Center district near the Veterans Memorial building. Their first landing probably was near the foot of Griswold. Fort Ponchartrain itself stood between Griswold and Shelby on the east and west, and between Larned and Woodbridge on the north and south.

Later the palisade was extended as far as Wayne Street which is near Washington Boulevard. The courer de bois working in the nearby forest drank the pure water of the little Savoyard river which once bordered the western edge of the palisade.

In the 1830's the Savoyard was covered over to become a part of growing Detroit's central sewer system. As Sam Johnson once said, "Life's a short summer, man a flower. He died, alas! How soon he died. Oh, catch the transient hour."

18. Ville d'Etroit Takes Shape as French Cut Dense Forest

Dense forest once surrounded the area we call the Civic Center and Hart Plaza. In 1701 hundreds of these trees were felled by Cadillac's men to build his La Ville d'Etroit, as he called it, and he built well and Detroit remained in French possession for six more decades.

CBS recently portrayed George Washington in a nationally televised "mini-series" in which Charles Stuart, a British officer, was shown in conference with Washington. This gentleman once was a captive in the stockade at d'Etroit.

The French had captured Stuart at Fort Duquesne (Pittsburg) in 1755 and even at that late date Detroit was not highly regarded by the British. After his release the next year Colonel Stuart wrote the English authorities:

"Fort De Troit is a stockade. They have no cannon mounted, but it is said they have one large gun in one of their stores. The fort covers about four or five acres of ground and contains about 70 houses which are built of logs and covered with board about an inch thick. They have no defense against bombs on the side next to the water. It is very weak and may easily be pushed down by men pushing against it. They have no earth works thrown up, nor liners for the seams, except some small stakes about five or six feet high."

Stuart's report of several pages was kept in the active file at the War Office in London and proved to be invaluable to the British later.

As far as Cadillac was concerned Fort Ponchartrain was a worthy achievement which he visualized as a private preserve—a kind of feudal seignorage with himself as the seigneur.

In fact, Cadillac petitioned for this privilege. The petition was filed in the archives of Paris and ignored by King Louis XIV and his minions. Louis thought that all of France belonged to him. "L'etat est moi " Cadillac chose to live like a seigneur anyway and he was ably seconded in this by the ambitions of Mme. Cadillac. These independent ideas ultimately would cost him his job.

Let's return to this manoir on the straits and see what they have built.

Without mechanical saws or horses, or any kind of special equipment, they have removed a forest of oak and other hardwoods, spiked one end of each log and sunk it into the ground around an area 200-feet square. Each palisade is at least 12-feet high. Inside they have built little houses of logs set upright like the palisade.

This construction was entirely by hard manual labor, day after day, for months. The French farmers and soldiers were helped in the work by the whole garrison, including the woodsmen (coureurs de bois) as well as the boatmen (the voyageurs).

The Indians, who also had a stake in the success of Detroit, worked as hard as anyone there.

When it was finished Cadillac pronounced it very good ("trés bon"). He named each bastion in honor of his Indian helpers. There was one "Bastion Potowatomi," and one for the Ottowa, and for the Huron, and the group the French called the Saulter who were the Ojibwa (Chippewa). They had come down from St. Ignace at Cadillac's invitation and built their own bark homes nearby.

Within the stockade were four main streets—St. Joseph, Ste. Anne, St. Jacques and St. Louis. A service street divided the square through the center.

At first all the little houses had dirt floors except the petite manoir of the Cadillac's and the church of Ste. Anne's and the priest's house. Each house had sod roofs supported by strong horizontal logs spliced into the vertical uprights.

At first the windows were of skins scraped very thin. Their first grain mill was copied from the Indian-style mill—a large round log in which a round hole had been burned. Over it a heavy pounder was attached to a spring pole. The corn was milled by this primitive method until a more modern mill could be imported.

The roofs of the little houses eventually blossomed with green, and the French painted their half-open, hospitable doors in the same color. The place had a charming ambience, colorful in the old French style with flower gardens in many yards.

They were a happy people. Music was an important part of their lives. They sang a lot. There were only two fiddles in the community, one owned by an old Indian who claimed he found it. The records say the other belonged to Jerome Martiac dit San Quartier who played the violin expertly and often was asked to perform at community dances. The dances began about eight and were known to last until four or five the next morning!

Every feast day was celebrated at Ste. Anne's, and Sunday was the day for dressing up. The peasant costumes of the week were cast aside and the people, especially the ladies, wore their best finery, outmoded versions of once-stylish

Parisian gowns. But they had esprit. The spirit of the place was a kind of lively joie d'vie. Underneath was a strong will to succeed in business and become a grand seigneur like Monsieur Cadillac

This human motif, which underlined all feudal cultures, is not unknown in today's twentieth century hurley-burley. But it had a different nuance in 1700.

Thomas Guerin in "Feudal Canada" states that some of the barons of old France came to America and became seigneurs. Some habitants of Quebec even today pay tithes in the old manner to these "nobles."

Guerin makes it clear that all the nobles in Canada became Seigneurs, but not all seigneurs were by any means noble. He cites the typical case of Noel Langlois, a hard-working, money-saving, excellent carpenter, who probably at the behest of his wife, decided to soar socially. By hard work and severe economies he managed to accumulate enough to buy some property at Port Joli. Once acquired, the semi-literate carpenter underwent a "sea change." After he reached the mountain top the good man put his tools away and became a particularly lazy, boozy "gentleman." C'est la vie!

Cadillac was of upper middle class stock but not of royal blood. He had married well. Some of his wife's family were closely connected with the court, and were said to be of "royal stock." And in France of that era that could mean a lot. Cadillac's father-in-law had made a fortune in the shipping business and, it was widely rumored, with some privateering on the side. Privateering means that he operated like a pirate, and it was said that young Antoine Laumet, as Cadillac was called in those days, was chief mate on the pirate ship.

These allegations found their way back to Fort Ponchartrain D'Etroit and they were no secret to the masses who bowed before my "Lord" Cadillac on tithing day in May. They must have worn an appreciative Gallic smile on their faces which really said, "I really know you, old man. You can't fool me. But we will play this game." Yes, indeed, there must have been a special understanding between Antoine and his "rentiers."

Now it is time to go down to the docks and watch the fleet come in.

Because it is wash day the dock of each little ribbon farm has hard-working women on it scrubbing on their wooden washboards, and cleansing their clothes in the clear waters of the Detroit River.

The dock on wash day was their home town radio center, TV station, and general clearing house for the news of the day. Sometimes their voices became excited and loud and the badinage was "telegraphed" to the neighborhood. By the time these story-tellers (échotiers) reached Ste. Anne's for a Sunday visit after church no one would recognize the original story, or even find a snippet of truth.

Let's watch the first boat arrive—a typical transport canoe. It's about thirty feet long, six feet wide with a crew of six, and capable of carrying a load of about 8,000 pounds. How would you like to paddle that from Montreal?

They unload at the special watergate of the fort. It is a secret load for Cadillac and goes immediately inside. We will tell you about that another time but, meanwhile, let's listen to the gossip of the women whose loud voices carry over the water from dock to dock with all the news of the day. Stay tuned.

19. Buried Facts Sometimes Obscure Cadillac's Story

Among the varied difficulties one encounters in the pursuit of truth regarding bygone happenings is the kind of blind obeisance many historians seem to pay to hearsay evidence.

Professor Harry Elmer Barnes in "A History of Historical Writing" states the case succinctly when he says, "the real historian is not the plodder or compiling clerk who gathers the facts from a diversity of sources. He is, rather, the one who takes this raw material, evaluates it, and organizes it in such a fashion as to illuminate our minds with respect to the nature of the past and the manner in which the past produced the present.

"It requires a far higher order of mind to produce historical synthesis than to carry on historical research, and it is for this reason that there are many research students and few real historians." This dictum certainly applies to one's pursuit of Sieur Antoine Laumet de La Mothe Cadillac.

No less a personage than Bruce Catton, whose "A Stillness at Appomattox" is one of the greatest stories of the Civil War I have ever read, produced a book he called "Michigan—A Bicentennial History."

With all due respect to Catton I find that Cadillac's malfeasance was white-washed by omission. Not once is any attempt made to reveal his true character, nor is one allowed to assume that Cadillac was anything less than an organizational genius and a highly moral leader of men. The same whitewash brush is used by many others in their so-called histories of Michigan.

The late Professor F. Clever Bald of the history department of The University of Michigan comes closer to the truth in "Michigan in Four Centuries," when he wrote:

"Besides being commandant of the fort and having the trade monopoly, Cadillac wanted to be the seignior of the region; that is the feudal landowner. Noblemen or other prominent colonists in Canada received large estates called seignories. In return, the seignior had to perform the ceremony of pledging fealty and homage to the king. Appearing at the Chateau St. Louis in Quebec before the governor as His Majesty's loyal representative, a seignior removed his hat and on his knees swore to be the king's loyal vassal.

"The people to whom the land was granted were called 'habitants.' They owed the seignior the ceremony of fealty and homage; they must raise their hats to him and stand in his presence; they had to take their grain to his mill and pay one-fourteenth of it for the grinding; they must agree to work a certain number of days each year on the seignior's farm and they were charged rent, which they usually paid in produce because coins were very scarce."

Cadillac never received a seigniory but he was permitted to grant land along the Detroit River and to collect rent. He took full advantage of this option.

The ordinary house lot within the stockade was no more than twenty-five feet wide. During the early years Cadillac distributed to settlers sixty-eight small lots within Fort Pontchartrain and about seventy-five ribbon farms nearby.

The ribbon farms were like those which lined the St. Lawrence River at Montreal and Quebec. At Ville D'Etroit they varied in width from one arpent (about 192.25 feet) to five arpents and ran back into the wilderness a mile or more.

From the beginning Cadillac had serious trouble with his "rentiers." Complaint was made to the governor in Quebec that Cadillac was overcharging them at the mill. They were paying one-eighth instead of one-fourteenth for grinding. And Cadillac required that each habitant pay rent in furs or in cash, and pay for the "privilege" of trading or working as skilled craftsmen.

Cadillac built a windmill on the river and upped the fees for grinding corn, a staple of the residents diet.

Cadillac had cattle and horses sent overland from the area of LaChin and Montreal.

The cattle thrived and multiplied but two of the three horses died. The one surviving horse, which Cadillac christened "Colin", was rented out to the habitants at very high fees.

There were so many marauding wolves that the pigs that were brought in with the cattle were threatened with extermination. For safe keeping they were removed to Belle Isle, which they called Isle aux Cochons or Hog Island. The island also was home to a large tribe of Ottawa among whom were the ancestors of Chief Pontiac.

To his friend in Paris, Count Ponchartrain, praised the little Ville D'Etroit extravagantly. He said, "The banks of the river are so many vast meadows where the freshness of these beautiful streams keep the grass always green.

"These same meadows are fringed with long, broad avenues of fruit trees which have never felt the careful hand of the watchful gardener; and fruit trees, young and old, droop under the weight and multitude of their fruit, and bend their branches toward the fertile soil which has produced them."

He waxed poetic as he described the area as "so temperate, so fertile, and so beautiful that it may justly be called the earthly paradise of North America." And he added, "winter, according to the savages, lasts only six weeks at most." (This may have been written before he survived a Michigan winter.)

The truth is that Detroit did not grow rapidly at first.

The word went forth that it cost too much to live there. Some even said that Cadillac was in league with some rough coureurs de bois to trade brandy for furs and debauch the Indian.

Others among his enemies said that Cadillac had delusions of grandeur and treated the habitants like slaves in a feudal society, keeping the lion's share of all the profit for himself.

His enemies persisted in their accusations and the Court at Versailles began to worry. The English in league with the Iroquois were pushing westward and the French were very concerned about holding their Fort Ponchartrain.

20. Heavy Boat Traffic on the River— Detroit's Main Street

The main stem at Detroit in 1700 was not a road but a river, and heavy traffic marked its passage night and day.

When evening came the river came alive with the sounds of life after dark—the music of the night. Many Indians came gliding by, headed for their camps or their favorite fishing places.

Overhead was the occasional whistle of a crane or the call of a dove. In the background was heard the staccato chop of thousands of fish jumping in the shallows along the shore.

From the fort nearby we hear the sound of a violin and the insistent pounding of a dozen feet dancing a French roundel. Occasionally a bateaux loaded with merchandise would slip in through the watergate at Ponchartrain.

South of the fort there is another rhythm somewhat alien to the music of the violin.

The sound is a primitive, insistent pounding of an Indian drum. This tom-tom beat is echoed and re-echoed to and from a camp across the river. What does this mean? Is it peace or war?

We are hearing the drums of the Potowatomi from their camp about where the Ambassador Bridge crosses the river today. They are signalling to their friends, the Hurons, who live directly across the way where the bridge enters Canada.

The Hurons are Iroquois and the "Pots" are Algonquin. How can these two traditional enemies find so much to talk about? For many years they have enjoyed a kind of drumbeat communication that seems to be meaningful to both of them, but no white man, as far as I know, has ever translated it. Maybe its only purpose is just friendship, communication, peace. And it worked!

When the Iroquois of the Lake Ontario region invaded this territory the Hurons were forced to flee, and they found shelter with their Potowatomi neighbors across the river. That is how the Hurons came to settle in the valley of the Rouge.

Cadillac wrote to his king, Louis XIV, in 1701:

"We have fish in great abundance, and it could not be otherwise, for this river is enclosed between two lakes." (The Cadillac papers may be found in Volumes 33 and 34 of the Michigan Pioneer and Historical Collection). Cadillac's inventory showed more than 1,050 barbed fish hooks, and they were not all for barter. Every day the runabout canoes, or piroques, of the French were out on the river fishing for their supper. The piroques were dug-out canoes made of logs and were in daily use for traveling between the little ribbon farms and the fort.

Bateaux, large flat-bottomed boats, were used for transport. Often one Frenchman in a piroque would be towing a bateaux loaded with farming tools and seeds.

Cadillac's river, the old records say, had more fish of a greater variety than any other place in the world. It teemed with salmon, muskelonge, wall-eyed pike, catfish, bass and dozens of other varieties. It was not uncommon for the Indians, who spearfished more than they used hooks, to impale two or three fish with one stroke. Gill nets also were commonly used.

At dawn the marshland air was filled with the rushing wings of thousands of birds. The settlers' records speak of a sky alive with the morning sound of singing birds. Cadillac wrote, "Game is very common as there are wild geese and all kinds of wild ducks. There are swans everywhere. There are quails, woodcocks, pheasants. There are so many turkeys that twenty or thirty could be killed at one shot. There are partridges, hazel hens, and a stupendous number of turtle-doves.

"I have seen birds of rare beauty. Some have a plumage of beautiful red fire color, the most vivid it were possible to see. I have seen others all yellow with tails bigger than their bodies and they spread out their tails as the peacocks do. I have seen others of a sky blue color with red breasts. There are many cranes, grey and white; they stand higher than a man. The savages value these greatly on account of their plumage with which they can adorn themselves."

Before we leave the river we must interview the gossiping Indian women washing on the dock.

What is the story of the day? It's the impending arrival of Mme. Cadillac and Mme. deTonty. They are coming from Montreal with their children and plan to make their home in Ville d'Etroit or so the story goes. Why would they leave the luxuries of their own manors to live in this wilderness, one wonders. To be with their husbands, one replied. Another one said, it is to give the lie to the Jesuits who have said that this place is not fit for man or beast.

What is she like, this Mme. Cadillac? "I'll tell you. She is greedy like he is. I knew her in Ste. Ignace. She got control of a boatload of furs from an old Indian who did not intend to give them away. A shrewd trader that one. Sharper than he. Watch out for her."

"I don't believe it," another one said. "She has a lovely face. Not evil that face."

And so the wild speculations went, on and on. Half-truths, more lies, repeated over and over. How much did they know? How much did they really believe? Time well tell.

In September 1702, Cadillac wrote to the court, "Be convinced, My Lord, that I have never had in view anything save the propagation of the Faith, the glory of the King, the care of his interests, and the benefit of the colony."

And, Cadillac continued, "How can these barbarians be made Christians unless they are made men first? How can they be made men unless they are humanized and made docile? And how can they be tamed and humanized except by their companionship with a civilized people? How bring them into subjection and make them subjects of the King, if they have neither docility nor religion nor social intercourse? All that can be done easily by the means set forth in my memorandum; and in perfecting the settlement of d'Etroit I have done for my part all that is necessary. It remains on yours to carry out what you have promised me."

But Louis XIV did not because he could not afford the expense. He did not give Cadillac absolute control or the supplies he had promised. So trouble brewed in paradise.

21. Many Fine French Families Called Ville d'Etroit Home

Across the years since 1701 there have been many changes in the city by the strait. Almost three centuries have passed since Ville d'Etroit danced to Cadillac's tune, yet the melody lingers on.

Even today many areas of Detroit have a distinctly French charm and ambience. Read the bronze historical markers, the street names and the phone book, and you will perceive that this town from the sidewalk cafe at the Regent on the Boulevard to the Ponchartrain at the RenCen still has a French flavor.

November 29, 1760, Major Robert Rogers and his Rangers took over Detroit and hoisted the British flag from the flag-staff at Fort Ponchartrain. Does that mean that he had conquered the place? Not really. The town remained essentially French.

The British, who wished to conduct a business or communicate with the people, soon discovered that they had to learn a second language. For many years Detroit was a bilingual town.

Even as late as the 1830s Father Gabriel Richard, the priest at Ste. Anne's, conducted services in French as well as Latin. Richard was Michigan's representative in Congress and had a bill passed for the construction of a road from Detroit to Chicago. This road now is Route 112 and follows the Sauk-Potowatomi Trail. All his life the good Richard spoke English with a French accent but he had the support of Protestant and Catholic alike.

The little ribbon farms on both sides of the river in Cadillac's domain gave street names to both Detroit and Windsor, and the descendants of these early French are among some of the prominent residents today.

Among these distinguished names the genealogist may find descendants of: Baby, de Rainville, Barthe, Beaufait, Campeau, Palms, Champoton, Piquette, DeQuindre, de-Beaubien, St. Aubin, Robert, Catin, Chene, DeMerles, Riopelle, D'Armour, DeJoncaire, Godefroy, Moran, Cicotte, Navarre, Visger, Audrain, De StLeger, Barron, DeBondy, DesNoyers, D'Armous, Riopelle, Dubois, Brisbois, Gamelin, DeMontag, Reaume, Gouin, Morand, DeBurros, Valliler, Vissier, Lafoie, Lefebre, Campau, Livernois, Cadieux, Cailerier, Beaujers, DeBonne, Chabert, Visger, St. Martin, Bourassa, Pelletier, St. Louis and many, many others.

These people were, for the most part, charming, hospitable, intelligent, energetic and artistic. They had a special French flair for living. Today many of their descendants are among the most productive, cultured, knowledgeable citizens of this area.

Our main concern, however, is not an account of the present but to develop an understanding of the past. The real story of Detroit must begin with its founder, Antoine Cadillac.

So let us return once more to the village on the strait for one last look before we face the incoming tide of the English and Rogers' Rangers.

Let us avoid the dreary drudgery of a detailed account of Cadillac's iterminable quarrels with the Jesuits, and his endless arguments with the Company of the Colony, the governing body in Quebec. Nor will we pursue his tedious battles with some of the French colony at Ville d'Etroit.

Those who wish to pursue these quarrels in all their savage fury may find the details in Volumes 33 and 34 of the "Michigan Pioneer and History Collection," and much more data may be found at the Burton Historical Library, and in the libraries of The University of Michigan.

I have gleaned many facts from these sources, and now I return to the picture as I have visualized it.

Two large transport canoes silhouetted in the crisp autumn moonlight ripple the water with a moon-spattered wake. They slip into the watergate at Fort Ponchartrain.

It's a beautiful night. Except for the moon, the only light is from a fading campfire across the river at the Huron's place. They must all be asleep by now. As the big canoes approach the dock the voyageur pilots signal for a quiet landing. The paddles are dragged in the water to slow the momentum of the boats.

On the dock we see two shadowy figures who seem to be struggling with a lock. One of these men looks vaguely familiar. He moves with great energy and purpose. Is this the commandant? Why would he conceal two boatloads of furs? My lord, it's three o'clock in the morning.

We make note of all this and add it to a small mountain of evidence we have accumulated. At last we think we may know the truth. Our brief indicts Cadillac.

The evidence indicates strongly that Cadillac's bete noire was greed—unholy greed. It detracted from his many good qualities and ultimately ruined his life. He was fired from his post at Detroit because of it, and later the same curse ruined his chances to leave a good record as Governor of Louisiana. When he died his life was embittered and sad.

But there was another side to Cadillac. He had many excellent qualities, superior ability, great energy and ambition. He achieved much in his long life, and although ruthless in business matters, he seemed religious in a conventional way.

First he built a warehouse, but within the week the foundations were laid for the church he called Ste. Anne's. And it stands today, a marvelous monument to the past—the oldest Catholic parish in the United States except one. That one is the cathedral in St. Augustine, Florida.

Cadillac was a loving father and a good parent. He and his attractive wife had thirteen children. The last six were all born in Detoit between 1702 and 1710.

The feeding and caring of this family was a heavy responsibility for the devoted parents. They had several Pani (Indian slaves) and one of them, an independent old fellow, may have been a spy for the British.

I have seen a copy of the Cadillacs' marriage certificate and his bride, Marie Thereze Guyon, was a daughter of Denis Guyon and Elizabeth Boucher. The Bouchers were distantly related to royalty. Cadillac gave his age on June 25, 1687, as twenty-six, and Thereze said she was seventeen. Other evidence indicates that he was somewhat older and she may have been only sixteen.

Her father was a relative of a prominent ship owner with whom Cadillac had once served as a ship's captain. Their ship was extensively used in privateering exploits along the coast, and with the profits from some of these forays Cadillac had acquired a plantation at Port Royal. The marriage certificate was signed LaMothe Launay. This is the name he used in his seagoing days.

A true Gascon, sharp-tongued and proud, quick to draw his sword, a great talker, a splendid writer, Cadillac was a remarkably clever man. However, I would not include straight dealing and generosity among his assets. Yet he seemed to be honest with the Indians. Was it because he was surrounded by them? At one time it was estimated that he had brought in more than 3,000 in the settlements around the fort.

When the French government refused to send him all the troops he needed to face a probable attack by the English, and the Iroquois, Cadillac called a pow wow with his Indian friends. His method of dealing with them indicates a keen understanding of their ways.

One day he invited a group of chiefs to dine at his table and he proposed a training school for a hundred warriors. He treated them with great courtesy and gave them many presents including wampum and tobacco, vermillion to paint their faces, ruffled white shirts and gorgeous red coats trimmed with gold French lace. He also included silver bangles, calico for the squaws, and, best of all, lots of French brandy.

Cadillac had no trouble getting Indian enlistments in his army, and he received many fine furs from the chiefs. The picturesque scene which has been cited in many old histories of the time went something like this: Cadillac addressed the chiefs as "My Children," and they called him "Father." Sitting around the fire with them he smoked the calumet as it passed from hand to hand. Then he employed the figurative language which the Indians understood and expected in diplomatic negotiations. Cadillac said, "I had lighted a great fire here. I had planted four great trees near this beautiful fire, two on my right hand and two on my left." He is referring to the villages of the Ottowa, the Potowatomi, the Huron and the Chippewa, which are near the Fort.

Then, when he had their rapt and friendly attention, he invited them to join the French Army. They honored this invitation and kept their word long after the British arrived. But that's another story.

Because Cadillac knew how to deal with the Indians, and respected their customs, they respected him. He and his family always were safe and cared for by the Algonquin of d'Etroit.

22. Cadillac Faces Government Inquiry

Five prosperous years for the little village on the strait followed its auspicious beginning on July 24, 1701. Then in 1706 its first citizen and founder was peremptorily summoned to Montreal for the third or fourth time. He had to face a serious inquiry into the operation of d'Etroit. A quasi-governmental group who called themselves "The Company of the Colony of Canada" demanded that Cadillac give an accurate accounting of his profits and losses. In as much as "The Company" was a competitor of Cadillac's in the fur market, it is a little like Ford Motor calling up General Motors and saying, "Now, boys, let's get together on this thing and corner the market." Cadillac wanted exclusive right and control of his own bailiwick, and he insisted upon his "rights." It was a long fight, and ultimately it caused Cadillac to be "kicked upstairs" by the government and made governor of Louisiana. But this did not happen until 1710, or thereabouts. He left in 1711. Cadillac won the first round in 1705 and returned from Montreal in 1706 with the reins firmly within his grasp.

Before we attend Cadillac's trial and examine the charges against him let us visit the little village once again to try to discover what life was really like for those early Detroiters.

During those first five good years everyone was required to perform his share of the work.

Cadillac made short shrift of idlers. They were warned and then, if they did not get the message, were jailed in a kind of makeshift bastille at one end of a warehouse, or were expelled from the colony. Cadillac did not fool with laggards.

Soon the little farms dotted the landscape almost as far north as Cadieux Road and on what today is called Windmill Pointe stood a remarkable, old-style French windmill. This area was called Cote d'nord.

Almost every farmer had his own dock and his little runabout canoe. Some of them lived at the fort and the river was their only highway home. In the beginning there were no roads outside of the little streets within the Fort Ponchartrain complex.

Stretched out in the sun on both sides of the river Cadillac looked out on a domain that was prosperous and growing. And the river was dotted with many canoes and bateaux, and people enjoyed plenty of fresh fish from its crystal pure waters.

The little farmers and sometimes their wives and children were laboring most assiduously in their vineyards and gardens. After food for themselves their produce went to the common market and to Cadillac who retained a percentage of everything raised.

Cadillac knew that the farmer, like the voyageur and the coureur de bois, were vital to the survival of his settlement, but in the structured society of that time and place they were rated far down the social scale.

Some who owned their farms in "fee simple" were considered a cut or two above the rest. It was not unknown in France to denigrate the peasant. This contributed to the French Revolution. This demarcation created some conflict in early Detroit.

May 1 was a day of celebration in Cadillac's country.

In 1702 the spring marked the arrival of Madame Cadillac and Madame Tonty, the wife of Alphonse Tonty, Cadillac's aide. On May 1 the villagers erected a Maypole in Cadillac's yard and amidst much rejoicing, wining and dining, they celebrated the arrivals of the ladies who were the first white women to take up residence in the state of Michigan. This May Day custom was followed for many years.

The ladies left Montreal in late summer. October seemed unusually windy that year and there was no assurance that the new treaty with the Iroquois would hold. Mme. Cadillac had two of her children with her and Mme. Tonty also had her children on board.

And so it was thought to be protective of the children and others to wait over with friends at Fort Frontenac (Kingston) until spring. It was suggested that they go the voyageurs route via the Ottawa River and Georgian bay, but with thirty or more portages and a heavy load of trade goods and clothing that highway seemed impracticable. So they waited until spring.

To friends at Fort Frontenac who tried to influence Mme. Cadillac and prevent them from going at all she is alleged to have said: "Do not waste your pity on me, dear friends. I know the hardships, the perils of the journey, the isolation of the life to which I am going; yet I am eager to go. For a woman who truly loves her husband has no stronger attachment than his company, wherever he may be."

This is a fine speech and is widely quoted in a dozen books about the Cadillacs; however, knowing her acumen in business affairs and Cadillac's total trust of his wife in his various and sometimes shady business dealings with the coureurs de bois and others, I am reasonably confident that she was fully aware of the current political situation as it affected her husband and their life together.

That first year when Cadillac had been granted his first rights in Detroit, King Louis XIV also granted vast rights to a group of merchants from Paris, Quebec, and Montreal who had banded together to corner the fur market.

This was the "Company of the Colony of Canada." They were as greedy as Cadillac had ever thought of being. When most of the Indians of Michilimackinac and St. Ignace flocked to Cadillac's banner—it was said that as many as 6,000 came to Detroit—the Governor of New France and chairman of the Company of the Colony, one Chevalier de Callieres, closed the fort at St. Ignace and burned it down. He left a skeleton crew at Mackinac.

The Jesuits had a vested interest in their mission at St. Ignace and Callieres decision damaged their prospects. Their dislike of Cadillac had grown since the old days when they had tried to bring Christianity to the Indians of St. Ignace and to curb their fondness for liquor.

The Company was so disturbed by Cadillac's success that they determined to bring him to a trial of his peers. But first they had to raise an excuse for a trial. False rumors were spread and like many invented stories they grew with what they fed upon.

If you believed these tales you would be afraid to go to Detroit because it was said to be a den of "wild, licentious, immoral" people held together by one Cadillac who was a "thief." The tale grew with each telling. The climate of Detroit became "unbearable." The cost of living there "prohibitive." Many people believed the stories and the emigration to the little fort on the straits fell off considerably.

Cadillac was very anxious to have his wife and Madame

Tonty come to live at the fort so he might prove it was a safe place for women.

Mme. Cadillac knew the motives of the people who were slandering her beloved husband, and she was as anxious as he to make her home at Fort Ponchartrain D'Etroit. Everyone was overjoyed when they finally arrived.

The May Pole celebration began and the Indians and whites rejoiced together. The ladies were treated with genuine respect and affection and no harm ever came to them. Later that year many other wives and mothers came and the lie was given to the concocted story that Detroit was "unsafe."

Let us return to the celebration in front of the manor house of the Cadillac's. It is an exaggeration to call it a manor—a simple place made of logs and only slightly larger than the other hovels that surround it. But the spirit of grandeur was there, and my liege Lord Cadillac and his charming wife greeted the happy throng with warmth and enthusiasm.

Some followed the feudal tradition and bowed before the man to whom they paid rent in furs or in cash for the privilege of living under the dubious shelter of Fort Ponchartrain.

What a handsome figure Cadillac and his officer made. Dressed in regimental blue with white trim and bright epaulets on their shoulders. Fine swords hung at their sides. And there also was the good priest of Ste. Anne's in his best long black robe. From a cord at his waist hung a magnificent silver cross. This was civilization on the strait in the year of our Lord 1702.

23. More Views of Old d'Etroit—a French Village on the Frontier

Visible on a clear day from the highest bastion at Fort Ponchartrain d'Etroit were the low hills off to the west that marked the banks of an ancient lake. Several branches of a primordial river that the French called the Rouge were clearly visible in the distance. And the landscape was streaked with the little streams which fed the hungry Rouge. Near a patch of meadowland surrounded by a grove of elm, willows, and a few poplars and ironwood trees was a persistent little rivulet the pioneers of a later day called Tonquish Creek.

Old Chief Tonquish was probably sixty or more in 1819 when he was shot by Captain Macomb and the militia from the fort. The event occurred as he neared Nankin Mills where a branch of the Rouge twists and turns along what we today call Hines Drive. In spite of the larceny that was known to dwell in the heart of Chief Tonquish, many pioneers wanted to honor him in death. So they called the meadowland near that place Tonquish Plain, and the little rivulet that met the Rouge near there was called Tonquish Creek. And so they remain to this very day.

Looking toward the northwest from the top bastion of the fort we can see beyond the swamplands the lovely St. Clair waterway. To the west of the ribbon farms along the river in the far distance is a beautiful area dotted with lakes and a forest of oak. Today we call this Oakland County in memory of the oak groves, some of which still survive.

Now it is time to narrow our perspective from the distant view to look upon the people scurrying here and there into the fort. Since Cadillac founded Ville d'Etroit in 1701 Fort Ponchartrain has been the center of this community's life and never more so than today May 1, 1702. On Cadillac's orders all three gates are wide open and hundreds of people are trooping in to celebrate the arrival of Mme. Cadillac and Mme. Tonty—the first white women to live in this state.

Standing with Cadillac on the porch of the small manoir that was their home as long as they lived in d'Etroit is his charming wife, and the Tonty's and the officers of the fort, and the black robed priest of Ste. Anne's. How Cadillac's golden epaulets glisten in the sun as does the handsome sword at his side! On this occasion Antoine Cadillac looked every inch the lord of his own demesne, and like King Louis XIV he could almost say, "L'etat, c'est moi."

Almost, but not quite. Let us consider the people—the masses who will judge their rulers and ultimately determine their fate. In the years following 1701 Cadillac made several trips to Montreal and Quebec to try to secure his colony on the strait. Every May Day the gates were open and the people came to pay their tithe and enjoy the free wine and hospitality of the Cadillacs. But in the hearts of this crowd there were many who were jealous of his success. And there were threats from the powers at Montreal and Quebec to close the place down. The Company of the Colony, the quasi official governmental body in Montreal, was planning action against d'Etroit. In addition there was the mounting threat of a British invasion, and the imminent danger of attack by the Iroquois who were goaded on by the British. And, perhaps worst of all, the Tontys, their erstwhile friends, had secretly joined the faction working against the Cadillacs. So the evil forces of jealousy and greed stalked the little village and swept many into its devilish net. There must have been some perceptive, sensitive people in that throng of May Day celebrants who knew this and realized that they were dancing on a tinder-box—a boiling cauldron of conspiracy and hate.

The years go by and the May Day custom remains. In 1704, just before the trial in Montreal, there was a particularly joyous party at the Fort. Look at the people as they stream in to get their free wine and free food. Some of them now realize the price they are paying for the entertainment. What a picturesque lot they are! Among the ladies we observe beautiful gowns in charming, Parisian styles. Their carefully coiffed hair is curled and dressed in the manner of Mme Maintenon, the mistress of Louis XIV, who, it is said, is the real mistress of the King's heart as well as of the palace at Versailles.

Not to be outdone by their ladies, the men who accompany them have greased their hair with a mixture of pomade and French perfume. Frenchmen who spend many hours handling muskrat, skinning beaver, smoke-tanning buckskin, plowing fields, or cleaning fish have need of French perfume, and any lapse in this direction would certainly be noted by their wives. The wives of the merchant class are more fortunate for their well groomed husbands are the leaders of the little community.

According to Calvin Goodrich in his remarkable "The First Michigan Frontier" the life of early d'Etroit was centered around the fort. All distances and locations in the region were spoken of in relation to it. The farm houses and buildings which dotted the shore line on each ribbon farm along the river were measured in terms of distance by canoe. The canoeing distance was so many arpents—an arpent was 192.25 feet long—from the flagpole at Ponchartrain.

Near the fort itself and the immediate area around the hub of activity in Cadillac's time were the homes of many settlers, the shops of the merchants and traders, a blacksmith shop, storehouses, gunpowder magazine, and, most important to many, the dear, little church of Ste. Anne's. And in this area too was the home of the Cadillacs, and the smaller house of the Tonty's, and the barracks for the soldiers. Another large building in the complex was the Council house where the weekly dances were held.

Behind them ran the Savoyard River which is now a part of the central sewer system of the city of Detroit. In the old days the Savoyard—named for a citizen of Savoy who built a pottery on its banks—rose in a swamp located about where Congress and Riopelle streets are today and crossed Woodward at Cadillac Square, flowed west below Congress, emptying into the river at Fourth street. It was deep enough in those days for canoes and bateaux to go up as far as Woodward.

Perhaps to many it may seem improbable that the people of frontier Detroit had any fun. Was it all work and no play? Of course not. The joyous heart and mind of the French native transcended his circumstances and he invented many happy recreational activities. For instance, he borrowed a rough game of kickball which the Indians had invented and called it lacrosse. It is still widely played in Canada. When the Indians played it, it was something like a cross between football and tennis. They had goal posts at each end of the field and they used bats like tennis rackets to carry a deerskin ball the length of the field.

Another pastime that the pioneers enjoyed was canoeing. Sometimes they would paddle out to Belle Isle which the Indians called White Swan. It was used by the French as a place for pigs and cattle.There were no canals on it in those days and much of it was a vast swamp full of mosquitoes and rattlesnakes.

All winter long when weather permitted there was racing on the Rouge river. They used light sleds pulled by fast, Canadian ponies. Bets were often made on the outcome of these races.

The Grand Prix of the early days was the horse races in the streets of the town. The little log houses were built next to the street, and the narrow log sidewalks were only two feet wide so the Grand Prix of the 1700's was quite a hazardous undertaking, but enjoyed by all.

In winter coasting was popular and although there were no slides as in Rouge Park. Shelby Street from Jefferson to the river was a favorite coasting area. The sleds could be made to coast a third of the way across the river at this point.

Picnics were a popular pastime. Surprisingly enough, they were not held in the summer which was a worktime, but used as entertainment in the sometimes long and dreary winters. Bundled up in sable-lined cloaks, great beaver hats, and face masks, the jolly picnickers climbed into sleighs piled high with warm, buffalo robes. The usual picnic spot was the race grounds at the Rouge. Indian slaves built a fire and a deer was barbecued. Everyone brought his own knife to cut off the venison. Women used delicate, little knives with handles of mother of pearl or silver. Plenty of wine and good French bread with winter berries completed the menu.

Carriage or horseback rides were also part of their fun as

well as fishing on the river. After a road was built out to a place that was later called Woodbridge Grove it became a very popular picnic spot. When you are sampling your hot dogs at the Tiger's game you may consider that this place was once a favorite picnic grounds for Cadillac's people. In the spring wintergreen berries and sassafras were found on Navin Field or Briggs Stadium. In the fall the French gathered hickory, hazel, and beech nuts in this area, and in season they found blueberries, strawberries, raspberries and blackberries. They were all plentiful and free for the picking at Woodbridge Grove.

24. Detroit in Turmoil as the Cadillacs Leave

After Cadillac's enemies had finally succeeded in forcing his removal as commandant of Fort Ponchartrain d'Etroit, life in the little colony became a dreary struggle. Antoine Cadillac and his family departed from the city on the strait in 1711, and disorder, contention, and turmoil soon took over.

The town's few public buildings became dilapidated and overrun with Indians. In fact, within a very few years conditions had deteriorated to the point where the government in Paris had almost decided to close the place down, and perhaps abandon it altogether. The events which led up to these pitiful conditions are pertinent to our story. Let's examine them, one by one.

Alphonse di Tonty, French speaking Italian aide of Cadillac's who had come to Detroit with him in 1701, was a jealous, greedy man who privately coveted what Cadillac had accumulated. Because Tonty was his long-time aide and trusted friend, Cadillac made him acting Commandant of d'Etroit in 1704 while he went off to Montreal and Quebec to face the government's query.

Cadillac was arrested almost as soon as he arrived in Montreal, but the Governor General was impressed with him and reduced the penalty to "house arrest." When not appearing before the court, pleading his own case, he lived at the Governor's Chateau de Ramezay. (This building is still standing in Montreal, and through the intercession of a friend in the Ministère de l'Education I was able to visit there. From there, after a tour of the city, we spent some time with the "Archives Nationales Du Quebec" using a "laissez-passer" to this wonderful institution.)

To return to Tonty—his conduct during the two years while Cadillac was away was most reprehensible. Among Tonty's nefarious schemes, which he put into effect almost as soon as he took over, was to correspond with people in Montreal whom he thought were Cadillac's enemies. This was a serious mistake. He contacted the wrong people, and Cadillac eventually learned of his aide's true allegiance. But irreparable damage had been done. Tonty did not realize that Cadillac had as many friends as he had enemies, and the friends were in high positions of trust.

Tonty sold most of the gun powder in the storehouse to the Indians, and he sold furs from the warehouse and kept all the profit. An inquisitive habitant discovered that most of their gunpowder was gone. There was not enough left to defend the town with if the Indians should attack. He published this sad news in the community and near panic ensued. Fortunately, within a week of this discovery Cadillac returned triumphant. He had won his case. He proceeded to try to replenish the ammunition and to reassure the habitants that they were in good hands once again. But within a few months he returned to Montreal to try to negotiate a better settlement with the Company of the Colony.

January, 1706, found a big, blustering fellow in charge of Detroit. He was Etienne Venyard, Sieur De Bourgmont. His dissolute life was a town scandal. The gossip on the docks reached a staccato pitch when they spoke of Bourgmont and his paramour, a half breed who called herself Tichenet. And when trouble came Bourgmont ran away.

Trouble came one day when he refused to listen to a request by the Chief of the Ottowas who wanted revenge for the slaying of one of their tribe by a Miami Indian. This had happened before Cadillac left some years back, and Cadillac had turned the problem over to Tonty for settlement. Tonty had avoided the issue. So the patient old chief once again brought up the matter of the Miami. He couldn't have found a more unsympathetic listener that Sieur Bourgmont. In fact, Bourgmont refused to mediate and turned the old fellow out of the fort. This was too much after all those patient years, and so the very next day the Detroit tribe of the Ottowas, Cadillac's old friends, rose up in righteous wrath and slaughtered all the Miamis they could find. They succeeded in killing all but one who escaped into the fort. However, the young Ottowa braves followed right up to the outer barricade. They were shooting indiscriminately. The good priest of Ste. Anne's, Father Constantine del Halle, who was working in his garden outside the walls, was killed. In no time at all the entire community was up in arms, and so were the Indians. The nearby colony of Hurons joined their friends, the Miami. A small scale war suddenly began. Poor d'Etroit was in the middle of it. A battered old Fort, only about thirty troops, and not enough ammunition to withstand a seige. Bourgmont's bungling had created an untenable situation. What next?

Before Cadillac returned Bourgmont deserted his command, He and Tichenet, and their hoodlum friends tried to join the English in New York. They fled south to a place along Lake Erie they thought was safe. It was a swampy cove near what is today Port Clinton. But somebody in Cadillac's pursuing party thought they might go into that area. French troops surrounded the place, and attempted to take them by surprise. Instead, they surprised themselves. In fact, they were horrified by what they saw.

Bourgmont and Tichenet and the others got away somehow. All fled into the wilderness except one forlorn, young man who thought he would confess and rely upon Cadillac's mercy. This poor fellow told the truth, begged for mercy, and in so doing brought down upon himself the fierce wrath of Cadillac and most of the community.

This brings us to one of the most gruesome episodes in the history of the Middle West. Cannibalism was found in Bourgmont's camp. They were starving, trapped, weather bound and scared to death. So they drew lots and decided who could live. The man who didn't run away may have been next on the list. At any rate, he confessed to being a participant in this communal mayhem. He was returned to Detroit in chains.

Cadillac was shaken and nauseated by the horrendous discovery and probably didn't consider mercy. He immediately impaneled a "Council of War." It included six officers of the garrison and himself, of course. After a somewhat cursory trial, the details of which are too gruesome to relate, the victim was put to death before a firing squad. This was the first execution on record in Michigan.

Cadillac repaired his Indian fences by dealing kindly with the Ottowas, but somehow his prestige and authority had suffered. Nothing was ever quite the same again in ville d'Etroit.

Cadillac remained in command until September 13, 1710 when Charles Rignault—Sieur Dubuisson, took over.

Dubuisson's first official act was to appropriate Cadillac's property—both real and personal. He would not permit the Cadillacs to sell or dispose of any of their holdings. This very high-handed proceeding was not officially sanctioned by the governor-general in Quebec, but neither was it stopped.

Cadillac was kicked "upstairs" and made governor-general of Louisiana. He was never to return to Detroit, or to reclaim any of the property for which he had expended so much effort and ingenuity. It was a sad ending in d'Etroit for a brave, gallant, courageous old fellow.

Dubuisson soon met his Waterloo when more than a thousand Fox Indians descended upon Detroit looking for their old friend, Cadillac. He had invited them to settle there. The war with the Foxes is another story for a later date.

Let's go down to the dock and watch the salt boat come in from Montreal. Except for "Indian salt," a strange tasting melange, all the salt must be imported. They do not know that they are sitting upon one of the largest salt deposits on this earth—the white mines of Detroit.

We leave them now to dream of a better day. Allons enfants de la patrie! Le Jour de Gloire est arrivé!

Luther Samuel Livingston
1866–1914

Courtesy of Grand Rapids Library
Michigan Heritage Room

Son of Keziah Burton Lincoln
and Samuel Livingston
Grandson of Luther Lincoln and Keziah Williams
Luther Samuel Livingston was a distinguished
American Scholar and Head Librarian of the
Widener Library of Harvard University.
He was also a distinguished Book Critic,
Botanist and Horticulturist. In appearance
he is said to have closely resembled his
grandfather, Luther Lincoln, whose
courageous and pioneering life is the
subject of the next section of this book.

25. Luther Lincoln— Plymouth Pioneer Born in Plymouth Colony Massachusetts

Sometimes the old dreams are forgotten and the dreamers fade away. But there is one we should remember. A long, long time ago in 1825 there was a young man in our town named Luther Lincoln—a brave and hopeful man with a dear wife and two children.

I have chosen to resurrect Luther Lincoln because I think he is worthy of our remembrance. He should be remembered in this place because he helped to build it. He was one of the founding fathers of our town. And what is even more, I think, he should remembered because he was a human being with a mind and spirit unlike any other.

Luther Lincoln of Plymouth, Mich., 1825, was not unlike his great great grandfather Thomas Lincoln (1635) of Bare Cove, Plymouth Colony, Mass.

Both Lincolns were millers and farmers and neither was afraid to challenge the unknown. They were seekers, always looking for a better place—over the rainbow.

Before we begin the saga of Lincoln let us try to understand his "roots"—those intangible forces which can shape a man or a woman—a person. These forces are his heritage and sometimes they may govern his life and determine his destiny. So it was with Luther Lincoln.

There were Lincolns in Norfolk from time immemorial and their name was variously spelled. Among the variants are: Lenckhome, Lencome, Linckhorn, Linckhone, Linckorn, Lincoll, Limcolm, Lincolne, Lincon, Lincorne, Linckcolm, Linckhornew, Linkok, Lyncolm, Linkornen, Lyncolne, and Lynkon.

Some of the Lincolns were said to have been descendants of a distinguished family of Lincoln. Elizabeth de Clinton, the Duchess of Lincoln, took a particular interest in the Plymouth Colony, and her chaplain planned to accompany the Pilgrims to America. However that may be, our interests are with plain Thomas Lincoln, miller and farmer, of the area of Hingham, Norfolk, England.

Thomas came to America in 1633 or 1634 (authorities differ on the exact date) with his wife, two children, many neighbors, friends, and Lincoln relatives.

They risked their lives and all they possessed in a leaky, old ship which barely made it past the rocks in Charleston's harbor. But any harbor was better than the turmoil and trouble they left behind them in England.

The 1600s were not the most auspicious time to look for peace in this world. The interminable Thirty Year War was grinding away on the continent and England was wrestling with the intolerable tyranny of the Tudors. The high-handed policies of King James inspired the Pilgrims to look for a new life in a free land and so the Plymouth Colony was born.

James died in 1625 and his son and heir, Charles I, continued his father's policies and added a few nuances of his own. Charles, whose greed knew no bounds, thought little of finding devious ways of stealing from the public. He was blessed with his father's inflated notion of royal power and raised money by various nefarious means. He even went so far as to revise obsolete feudal laws so that he might collect from all who disobeyed. And he forced wealthy people to apply for a knighthood so that he could charge them exorbitant fees for their titles. He forced judges to increase fines and to arrest people on trumped-up criminal charges.

Then Charles levied taxes on ships and shipping—an outrage to every Englishman. He tried to force the Episcopal system of church government upon the Puritans and the Scotch Presbyterians. The result of all this was armed rebellion and the outbreak of civil war. January 30, 1649, was the end of the road for King Charles. Oliver Cromwell witnessed his execution on a common jail stand in front of his old Whitehall Palace. All England rejoiced except for a few diehard loyalists and their minions.

But long before this welcome event occurred the Lincolns of Norfolk had fled their familiar fields to seek peace in America. Thomas Lincoln and his family were in the vanguard of a group which left Hingham in the summer of 1633.

The Lincolns were a respectable, middle class family and the baptismal and property records of Hingham testify to this. They must have been pleased to have on board their ship the young Reverend Peter Hobart who was an intellectual, a scholar and a civic leader in the community. He graduated from the University of Cambridge in 1625. There were opportunities for Hobart even in King Charles' England, but he preferred the company of his townsmen and the freedom of America.

In June 1635 we find Hobart living in Charleston, Mass., and preparing to join the Lincolns and others of his old Hingham group at Bare Cove on the south of Massachusetts Bay. (Bare Cove was so-called because the rocks on shore were exposed at low tide). Under Hobart's leadership,- Thomas Lincoln and his friends drew for home lots on September 18, 1635.

There were twenty-six lots drawn and Thomas Lincoln was lucky in the draw. Granted an excellent location for a house lot and five acres for a farm and mill on the river, his land was near Main Street which today is called South Street. Later he added considerable acreage to his holdings.

Thomas Lincoln, highly regarded by the settlers, was a successful miller. Bare Cove became Hingham because Thomas Lincoln and Rev. Hobart and others wanted to remember their old home in England. The Lincoln mill, which was strongly fortified, was regarded as a safe place to be in event of another Indian raid. But the town did have an adequate blockhouse and a volunteer militia.

The town had four Thomas Lincoln's whom they distinguished by occupation: Thomas, the weaver; Thomas, the miller; Thomas, the husbandmen; Thomas, the cooper. All were related. So Hingham has many Lincolns today.

Thomas and his second wife, Elizabeth Harvey Strait (widow of Francis Strait) had seven children. Among them was Thomas, Jr. who was baptized by the Rev. Hobart on February 6, 1637.

Perhaps to meet the needs of his growing family, or perhaps as the result of some local dispute, Thomas moved his family and mill to Taunton before 1650. His will states that he was 80 in 1683, the year he died in Taunton. But he is not forgotten.

The town of Hingham, Plymouth Colony, has a lovely old Lincoln Street that leads down to the area where the mill used to be, and near there is a charming old house open to the public. It has been owned and lived in by nine generations of Lincolns beginning with Perez who settled in Hingham in 1633.

Another distinguished house in this old town is that of Samuel Lincoln, ancestor of Abraham. It was erected in 1807 and designed by Charles Bullfinch, a noted colonial architect. These places are well worth seeing. Another place I enjoyed is at 19 Lincoln Street, part of the "Ordinary," an ancient pub built in 1650. While you are there, look at the nearby cemetery which is the resting place for many Lincolns including Governor Levi, and old General Benjamin Lincoln of Revolutionary War fame.

So there always will be Lincoln memorabilia in Hingham, but we must follow our genealogical train a few miles to the southwest and the town of Taunton and its nearby town of Norton. That is where we will find Luther Lincoln and his family.

F. W. Hutt's history History of Bristol County states that the Lincolns (Thomas Sr. and Jr.) were among thirty-five persons who paid in 1652 some twelve shillings each to have the right to all future divisions in Taunton. The money was for public use and to "Extinguish" Indian titles.

Another old story, widely believed, is that King Phillip (Massasoit's son) and some sachems of his tribe met at Lincoln's mill in 1675 and passed the peace pipe. But it was to no avail. King Phillip's war was one of the bloodiest of that savage era.

Space and time limit our genealogical survey of the Lincoln family. We do know that President Abraham Lincoln descended from this family through Samuel and Mordecai, cousins of our Thomas Lincoln Sr. (Abraham's genealogy is the topic for another study.)

Miss Alice Wyman Lincoln of Medford, Mass. was an authority on the Thomas branch of the family and she traced Luther's descent as follows:

(1) Thomas Sr. (whose story has been outlined); his second wife, Elizabeth Harvey was the mother of Thomas Jr. (2) Thomas Jr. married Mary Austin and raised a large family in Taunton of whom (3) son Jonah or Jonathon, who died Jan. 1773 and left a son, (4) Luther who married Rachel Macomber, Feb 9, 1792 in Berkley; they had, among others, a son (5) Luther, Jr., who was born October 19, 1794 and was baptized May 19, 1803. This is our Luther Lincoln of Plymouth, Grand Rapids, and Lincoln Lake.

There is a record in Volume 22 of the New England Historic and Genealogical Record which states that Keziah Williams of Taunton married Luther Lincoln of Norton. The date of the marriage is not given. But because of other evidence and place, as well as the names, I feel certain that she is Lincoln's wife. The Lincolns named their daughter Keziah. Her mother's genealogy is clearly stated, going back to the Pierce, Eddy, and Williams families.

26. Luther Lincoln's Birthday Celebrated in Family Homestead

A golden October rimmed the ancient hills of Massachusetts, lighting the sky with the magical colors of autumn. But there was an obstinate chill in the air, and wispy trails of white smoke etched the sky from almost every chimney in the sleepy, little village of Norton. On this bittersweet day of October 19, 1794, there is a great bustling about in the Luther Lincoln household.

As we enter the hospitable old farm home we observe Luther Sr. on his knees in front of the fireplace in the "borning room." He is trying to coax a reluctant flame into some semblance of warmth for the comfort of his lady, Rebecca Rachel Macomber Lincoln, who is expecting another child.

According to the records, Rebecca Macomber had married Luther Lincoln in Berkley in 1792.

Their first child, a little girl, had lived only a few days. She appeared to be a healthy, perfect baby and her death was altogether unexpected. No one ever knew the cause. Today, nearly 200 years later, we don't know much more about what we sometimes label "crib death."

So now, a year later, there is an underlying anxiety in this household. Luther expressed deep concern by getting the best midwife in the area to come several days ago. She is Aunt Lucy, the most successful midwife in Taunton. Hundreds of babies in the area can thank her for their lives. Lucy has taken command of the Lincoln "borning room" and everyone is ushered out.

Grandmother Macomber is in the kitchen, disguising her anxiety with a kind of perpetual business. Luther is ordered to finish butchering the venison while grandma makes the apple butter and then settles down to her spinning wheel near the entryway so she can keep track of the activity in both rooms. Obstinate, determined, smart, this old lady can make everyone march to her tune.

Luther built the fireplace in the kitchen which has a fore-log and a backlog. All the furnishings are made of the best iron. There is a trammel with several notches, a swinging crane, excellent andirons, and a long-handled meat rack and several skillets and numerous pots and pans. There is even a floor toaster and a kind of Dutch oven and a large kettle in which the apple butter now is simmering. Another large kettle is for soap making. There are two tea kettles steaming on the hearth.

Aunt Lucy comes bustling in to announce that "all is well," and removes one tea kettle leaving the other one to steam on an iron trivet.

Hear that pounding at the woodshed door.

Luther answers it to a faithful Jobe, a helper at the mill, who comes stumbling in to inquire, "Has it happened yet?" He assures Jobe he will let him know as soon as he can. Jobe seems satisfied with this and heads back toward the river. Soon, in the distance, the old millstones can be heard—grinding again.

After another hour faint sounds from the borning room reach the kitchen. Grandma prays, silently. But the hours went by slowly, and it seemed to take forever. And forever.

Then came the sound. A lusty, healthy, howling cry that only a strong boy baby could make. Aunt Lucy greets Luther and grandma, "It's a boy, a healthy strong baby boy." And Rebecca was fine, so all is well.

The news is told to Jobe who rushes off to tell the men at the mill. "Let us rejoice and be happy. Luther says you may have the rest of the day off." And so they celebrated the birth of young Luther. And it came to pass that Luther Lincoln Jr. was safely ushered into this world and into the warm and comforting bosom of his family on October 19, 1794.

This is the same Luther Lincoln who later is to be one of the founders of Plymouth, Mich., and, eight years after that, one of the first residents of Grand Rapids, Kent County, and later one of the pioneers of Montcalm County.

But thirty years will pass before we find Luther Lincoln Jr. at the land office in Detroit where he applied for land in Plymouth, Mich., on November 5, 1824. His claim was validated before that of William Starkweather. Lincoln purchased two 80-acre parcels but the one which interests us most is in Plymouth.

That acreage is the west half of the northeast quarter of this area. He paid $100.00 for the 80-acre tract, or the equivalent of $1.25 per acre. The land is roughly bounded by the present Mill Street on the west, and by Riverside Cemetery on the east. It was a ribbon strip along the water which was ideal for the milling business. Luther operated a lumber mill and a grist mill here for seven years. But we are jumping ahead of our story.

Thirty years will pass from 1794 to 1824. What happened to Luther Lincoln and his family during that time, and what happened to the other people in his New England environment?

27. Thomas Lincoln
Meets King Philip

Among the traditions of the Lincoln family—the handed-down folklore that is a part of every family's acculturalization—may have been old stories about grandfather Thomas Lincoln and the mill.

One of the family tales revealed how in 1675 Thomas Lincoln and other local leaders negotiated a peace settlement with King Philip, the Indian chieftain who had declared war on all of white New England. The treaty hammered out at Lincoln's mill slowed the impetuous Philip for only a short time—about six months. But when Philip returned to the warpath his pace was more cautious. The Lincoln Mill Treaty probably paved the way toward the final peace.

The landmark Lincoln mill served the community for almost two centuries.

Solidly built of rugged old oak and other hardwoods, it was regarded by the people both as a mill and a meeting place. In emergencies it served as a blockhouse for those working nearby. Those who have been following this series may recall that the mill had been built about 1652 by great-great-grandfather Lincoln who was called Thomas, the miller, to distinguish him from three other Thomas Lincolns in the Hingham area. They were: Thomas, the cooper; Thomas, the husbandman; and Thomas, the weaver. All were believed to have been related

When Luther's Thomas left Hingham in 1652 he may have been seeking a more independent identity as well as more opportunities for the milling business. At the time he moved to Bristol County it still was a part of the old home base, the Pilgrim county of Plymouth.

The histories of that early period devote many pages to King Philip's War and many mention the Lincoln mill. Probably we cannot approach an understanding of this early time and its people without a survey of the Indian troubles of that time and place.

For fifty years the Plymouth Colony had enjoyed a peaceful coexistence with Chief Massasoit, ruler of the Wampanoags who lived between Taunton and Plymouth.

Massosoit also was the chief sagamore and overlord of the Indians on Cape Cod and all around Massachusetts Bay.

The Pilgrims also were befriended by Squanto, Samoset, Hobamack, and others. Governor William Bradford in his journal calls Squanto a "special instrument sent of God for their good, beyond their education."

One day Squanto walked the corn field with Captain Myles Standish and others showing them how to fertilize the soil with alewives (herring). Using his own private hoard Squanto placed an alewive in each hill of maize. This idea was new to the Pilgrims.

Bradford states that Squanto also was their pilot, "bringing us to unknown places for our profit." Other Indians showed them how to make a deer trap, and revealed where the best clams were and where the fish were hiding.

The truth is that our forefathers probably would have starved to death that first winter without the help and guidance of their Indian friends. Let us not forget that.

Chief Massosoit kept the peace for more than fifty years. He was an amiable, intelligent sagamore with confidence in the white man's purpose. However, this long span of peace largely may be attributed to the leaders of the Plymouth Colony itself. The men who wrote the Mayflower Compact were diplomats in their own right. Gentlemen like Bradford, William Brewster, Captain Standish, Stephen Hopkins, and the rest seemed to know intuitively how to deal with the Indian mind.

One day Chief Massasoit practiced a little diplomacy on his own.

He requested an audience with the Plymouth Court. He brought his two oldest sons, Wamsutta and Metacom, and asked the honorable court to change his son's names to English ones. With all due respect, and a lengthy time for a ponderous discussion, the Plymouth Court recalled the ancient kings of Macedon. They named Wamsutta-Alexander, and Metacom became Philip.

The genesis of these ancient names was explained to Massasoit and he seemed well pleased with the court's decision. The old chief must have been aware of the tremendous energy and the fierce, implacable anger in his sons. He probably hoped that by anglicizing their names they would become more conforming in their life styles.

Massasoit held them with a firm leash as long as he lived. He attributed their tendency toward rebellion to the spirit of youth. It has been said that he often prayed to his gods to help keep his sons within bounds. However, within a month of his death in 1661, all hell broke loose.

Wamsutta, the older son, succeeded his father and went to Plymouth with his brother Metacom to confirm a new treaty with the Pilgrims and to have their English names confirmed again.

A few months later it was learned that Alexander (Wamsutta) was plotting against the Pilgrims. So he was confronted at his hunting lodge near Taunton by Major Joseph Winslow and ten armed men who commanded him at pistol point to return to Plymouth.

While incarcerated in the Plymouth gaol he contracted a fever and suddenly died. This mysterious demise never has been entirely explained by the historians of that era. Alexander's twenty-four year-old brother, Philip, called his death "murder." Philip's rage, although somewhat concealed, knew no bounds. He vowed revenge, and he prepared for war.

28. King Philip Seeks Revenge For His Brother's Death

After Massasoit's death followed closely by his brother, Alexander's sudden and mysterious demise, King Philip found it necessary to resume negotiations with the English.

It served his purposes to acknowledge Plymouth's rule once again and to promise to pay 100 pounds for the privilege of living in the area. Philip also promised to present the Plymouth Colony annually with five wolves' heads. It further was stated that he would not dispose of any of his remaining lands without the approval of the governor of the Plymouth Colony. (For a full text of this agreement as well as many valuable clues as to Philip's real character, read B. B. Thatcher's "Indian Biography." This was first published by Harpers in 1832 and reprinted by the Rio Grande Press in 1973.)

Philip vowed revenge and made preparations for war and for thirteen long years Philip secretly traveled from tribe to tribe throughout New England. The burden of his message always was the same. "You have two choices," said Philip. "You may be overwhelmed by the Pilgrims, or you may kill them and throw their bodies into the sea. Take your choice, What is it to be?"

Standing tall in the majestic robes of an Indian King, his confident message had a powerful influence upon them.

Philip was more intellectual and more decisive than his brother; his people followed him without question. Eventually he won most of the Indians of New England to his cause.

The Christianized, so-called "praying Indians," remained loyal to Plymouth and so they were removed for their own protection to an island in the sea near Boston. There, in a kind of early concentration camp, they nearly starved to death.

Philip knew that he had to weld many divergent forces into one fighting unit.

Divided by the sword of tribal jealousies and the bones of old contentions it was no small feat to bring them together. Philip was resolute and unwavering in his search for revenge.

"You must burn every house, destroy every village, kill every white man and throw their bodies into the sea," he asserted. "Redeem your land, cleanse your fields. We are all one in this cause." He insisted over and over again that "our common enemy, our only enemy, is the white man."

How do we know what King Philip said and thought during those more than thirteen years from the death of his father (Massasoit) in 1661 to the opening of King Philip's War in 1675? The old journals and diaries of the time tell the story. The most relevant of the lot is William Bradford's "Of Plimouth Plantation" which is available to the public in several reprints. I also would recommend "Saints and Strangers" by George F. Willison, Professor Babette Levy's "Cotton Mather," Marion Starkey's "Land Where Our Fathers Died," and the "nose-to-ground" study by Kate Caffrey, "The Mayflower."

Among the facts we know is that there was a spy in Philip's camp. His name was John Sassaman and he was King Philip's right-hand man and most trusted aid.

Sassaman was a Christianized, English-speaking Indian and a bright student at Harvard College. He was used by Philip as an interpreter and personal secretary. Kate Caffrey quotes a letter from Philip to Governor Prince which is probably indicative of Sassaman's scholarship and Philip's spirit. Although set in lower case, and sometimes in phonetic spelling, it shows great style and subtlety:

"to th honoured governit, mr thomas prince, dwelling at plimoth. honoured sir.

king philip desires to let you understand that he could not come to the court, for john, his interpreter, has a pain in his back, that he could not travel so far and philip's sister is very sick. philip would entreat that favour of you, and of the magistrates, if any english or enjians speak aboute the land, he pray you to give them no answere at all. the last summer he made that promise with you, that he would sell no land in seven yeares time. he had not forgot that you promoted him. he will come as sune as possible he can speak with you, and so i rest. your very loving friend, philip, dwelling at mount hope nek."

Sassaman was secretly indebted to the governor of the Plymouth Colony. (Perhaps it was not a coincidence that this was the case.) At any rate, from time to time, the inner guard of the Plymouth Colony was fully informed of Philip's moves. When the chips were down and a serious attack upon the struggling Pilgrims seemed imminent, Sassaman went to the governor with most of the details of the conspiracy. A few days later Sassaman's body was found floating in a Plymouth pond.

The authorities immediately arrested three Wampahoags.

Philip protested vigorously, stating that they had no right to arrest his men for crimes committed by them against other Indians. The culprits were given a brief trial, found guilty, and the morning of June 8, 1675, found them swinging from the gallows in Plymouth park.

Twelve days later the word went forth from Philip's camp that it was war. Painted and feathered and ready for blood, a thousand young braves came whooping out of his base camp at Mount Hope with murderous fire in their brown eyes. They surprised nearby Swansea with a merciless attack, and like the hordes of Genghis Khan, killed every white in sight.

King Philip had his war and all New England was in a state of shock and near panic.

In no time at all the entire Connecticut River Valley was soaked in blood. Midnight raids were followed by daylight ambush. Massacre followed massacre. The terrified colonists battled back the best they could, but it was some time before they mounted an effective resistance.

Eventually every able-bodied man became a part of the militia, and most women who had guns knew how to use them. Some of the towns offered large bounties for Indian heads.

Philip's line was very tenuous and eventually he came up short in food, guns, and ammunition. He also faced desertions and, again, betrayal. His beautiful wife, who was a sachem in her own right, and his only son, were captured. Philip became despondent, and said: "My heart breaks. I am ready to die." His strategy suffered from his lack of thoughtful planning. Eventually he was cornered in a swamp where he was cruelly murdered by one of his own Indians. With his death August 11, 1676, his cause collapsed.

His wife and child were held in "protective" custody for some time. Then Cotton Mather and the court had several long sessions to determine their fate. It is a blot on Mather's record that he voted to kill them, but the Rev. Keith and some more liberal forces from Boston prevailed and they were allowed to live. The nine year-old son (Massasoit's only grandson) and his mother were packed on the slave ship to Bermuda with hundreds of other captives. It was a profitable business for the English settlers.

Before the war was over fifty-two of the ninety white settlements in New England had been attacked, of which twelve were totally destroyed.

The dead never were completely counted but they probably numbered more than a thousand on each side.

The settlers probably didn't realize it, but King Philip's War was the opening gun in a racial conflict which went on and on for two centuries. Perhaps the climax came on the western plains in the 1800s, but we hear overtones of it again and again, even today.

29. Three Indian Leaders Meet Strange and Violent Deaths

Although Luther Lincoln was not born until October 19, 1794, the story of King Philip's War and the desolation that followed it must have been a part of the Lincoln' family's folklore and conversational reminiscences. The old Lincoln mill was near one of King Philip's camps. Powwows and massacres, peace parleys and mayhem, occurred nearby. Norton and Taunton were near the heart of the troubled Plymouth Colony.

Far to the West in the Detroit area about 100 years after the time when King Philip's head was impaled on a pole on Fort Hill Road in Plymouth, Mass., (where it remained for nearly twenty years as a warning to all passing Indians) there appeared on the scene a remarkable young Indian chief the French called Pondiac or Pondiag. The English called him Pontiac.

His native Ottowa referred to him as Obwandiyag. According to Dr. Howard H. Peckham in his study "Pontiac and the Indian Uprising" (Princeton University Press), in Ottowa the name was pronounced Bwon-diac. And Obwon meant "his stopping." (No meaning has ever been discovered for "diac," but I am working on it. As a matter of fact, that will be one of the questions I will ask a head chief of the Ottawa with whom I have an interview next month).

In many ways the careers of these two strong native Americans, Philip and Pontiac, were parallel. Both were Algonquin in their language pattern and heritage. Both were leaders, men of great courage, above average ability, and both had a kind of determination to defend their people to the death. They both displayed an almost Herculean will to overcome the enormous forces against them. Both were betrayed and murdered by their own people.

On a smaller scale, Chief Tonquish also was a formidable opponent. He showed great courage and determination, and defended his people and his hunting ground to the end. When he went to his Sky Father it is said that he had a prayer on his lips bemoaning the death of his only son, Toga, whose slaughter he had witnessed.

There is a mystery surrounding the death and final burial place of all three of these chiefs. Somewhere in Section 4 in the Township of Nankin on some land once known as the Dimmick farm lies what is left of old Tonquish.

For the death of King Philip read George F. Willison's "Saints and Strangers." It is a brutal story of betrayal by a "Praying Indian" named Alderman. After Philip's head and hands were cut off, his body was quartered and left for the wolves. The head, impaled on a pike on Fort Hill Road for many years, became a white bleached skull.

According to Willison, it was a favorite resting place for wrens. Alderman somehow obtained possession of his right hand and preserved it in a pail of rum. For about seven years he went around the colony with his pail proclaiming himself a hero.

Pontiac was murdered by a Peoria Indian while visiting his friends among that tribe in Cahokia, Ill., near St. Louis.

There also is a mystery regarding his final resting place. At least five different burial spots have been thought to be the exact spot. On one of these, the DAR placed a bronze tablet, and on another the Missouri Historical Society placed a marker.

The truth is no one really knows where Pontiac is buried. All of the places under consideration in St. Louis occupy a rectangle 1,200 by 450 feet. All we know for certain is that his death occurred April 20, 1769.

I prefer to believe another story. Pontiac's good friend, Chief Minavanana, head of the Chippewa, came to Cahokia to seek revenge for Pontiac's assassination. Minavavana secretly removed Pontiac's body, brought it to Michigan where it was reburied in one of the favorite haunts of Pontiac's youth, Apple Island—a lovely spot in the center of Orchard Lake near the intersection of Long Lake Road and Pontiac Trail.

Address the author for additional copies:

Ms. Helen Gilbert
c/o Plymouth Heritage Books
P.O. Box 6315
Plymouth, MI. 48170

Bibliography

An inclusive bibliography listing every book I have read pertinent to this subject would be too lengthy for the prescribed limits of *Tonquish Tales*. For the reader's convenience this selected bibliography is divided topically according to the book's principal themes: (1) Early Indians, (2) Chief Tonquish, (3) Cadillac's d'Etroit, (4) Luther Lincoln.

The most important resources used in writing *Tonquish Tales* were:

1. Michigan Pioneer and History Collections (Forty Volumes) Hereafter referred to as MPHC.
2. Michigan History Magazine (Over Forty Volumes) MHM.
3. Almon E. Parkin. The Historical Geography of Detroit (Lansing, 1918).
4. Calvin Goodrich. The First Michigan Frontier (Ann Arbor, 1940).
5. Harlan Hatcher. Lake Erie (The American Lake Series, Indianapolis, 1945).
6. George R. Fuller, ed. Historic Michigan (Selections from M.P.H.C.).
7. F. Clever Bald. Michigan in Four Centuries. (N.Y. Harpers, 1954).
8. M. M. Quaife and Sidney Glazer. Michigan From Primitive Wilderness to Industrial Commonwealth (N.Y. Prentice-Hall, 1948).

Blackbird, Andrew J. History of the Ottowa and Chippewa Indians. Little Traverse Regional Historical Society, pub.

Blair, Emma H. Indian Tribes of the Upper Mississippi and the Great Lakes, Cleveland 1911.

Brandon, William. Book of Indians American Heritage, Pub. 1961.

Caruso, John Anthony. The Great Lakes Frontier. Indianapolis, 1961.

Claspy, Everett. The Potowatomi of Southwestern Michigan. Dowagiac, 1966.

Danziger, Edmund Jefferson, Jr. The Chippewas of Lake Superior. Univ. of Oklahoma, 1979.

Densmore, Frances. Chippewa Customs. Washington, 1929. Smithsonian Bureau of American Ethnology Bulletin.

Downes, Randolph. Council Fires on the Upper Ohio. Pittsburgh, 1940.

Edmunds, R. David. The Potowatomis, Keepers of the Fire. U. of Okla. 1978.

Foreman, Grant. The Last Trek of the Indians. N.Y. 1972.

Gilbert, Henry. C. (Head of Mackinac Agency 1850s which controlled all Michigan Indians). Private Papers, Detroit, and at Bureau of Indian Affairs, National Archives.

Greenman, Emerson F. "The Indians of Michigan" MHM. Vol. XLV 1961.

Hatcher, Harlan. The Great Lakes. Oxford Press, N.Y. 1944.

Hinsdale, Wilbert B. Archaeological Atlas of Michigan. Ann Arbor, 1931.

Hinsdale, Wilbert B. The First People of Michigan. Ann Arbor, 1938.

Hinsdale, Wilbert B. Primitive Man in Michigan. Ann Arbor, 1925.

Hoffman, Walter J. The Midewiwin of the Ojibwa. 7th Annual Report. Bureau of Ethnology.

Hodge, F. W. Handbook of American Indians. Pageant Books, 1959.

Huntington, Ellsworth. The Red Man's Continent. New Haven, 1920.

Indian Claims Commission N.Y. Garland Press 1974 (3 Vols.)

Jahoda, Gloria, Trail of Tears. N.Y. 1970.

Johnson, Ida Amanda. The Michigan Fur Trade. Black Letter Press, Grand Rapids 1971.

Kappler, Charles J. ed., Indian Affairs: Law & Treaties. Washington, 1904.

Kellogg, Louis Phelps, ed., Early Narratives of the Northwest. New York. 1917.

Landes, Ruth. The Prairie Potowatomi: Tradition and Ritual. Madison, U. of Wisc. 1970.

Landes, Ruth. The Ojibwa Woman. Columbia U. Press. 1938.

McDonald, Daniel. Removal of the Pottowattomie Indians from Northern Indiana. Plymouth, Ind., 1899.

McKenney, Thomas Lorainne. Sketches of a Tour of the Lakes. Baltimore, 1827.

Matson, Nemiah. Memories of Shaubena. Chicago. D. B. Cooke & Co., 1878.

O'Callaghan, Edward. New York Colonial Documents. (See Index) Albany, 1853.

Parkman, Frances. France and England in North America. 2 Vols. Boston, 1896.

Prucha, Francis Paul. American Indian Policy. Cambridge, 1962.

Quaife, Milo Milton, Chicago and the Old Northwest. Chicago, 1913.

Quaife, Milo Milton. Lake Michigan. Indianapolis, 1944.

Quimby, George Irving. Indian Life in the Upper Great Lakes. U. of Chicago Press, 1960.

Quimby, George Irving. Indian Culture & European Trade Goods. U. of Wisc. Press, 1966.

Royce, Charles C. (comp.) "Indian Land Cessions in the U.S." 18th Annual Report of the Bureau of American Ethnology, Washington, 1899.

Satz, Ronald D. American Indian Policy in the Jacksonian Era. Lincoln, U. of Nebraska, 1975.

Schoolcraft, Henry R. Historical and Statistical Information, Indian Tribes. . . . Philadelphia, 1851.

Schoolcraft, Henry R. Narrative Journal of Travels from Detroit Northwest through the Great Chain of Lakes . . . in the year 1820. (Albany, 1821).

Stevens, Frank E. The Black Hawk War. Chicago, 1903.

Tanner, John. A Narrative of the Captivity and Adventures of John Tanner. Facsimile of 1830 ed. Minneapolis, 1956.

Thatcher, B. B. Indian Biography. N.Y. 1832. Reprinted 1973 by Rio Grande Press.

Tiedke, Kenneth E. A Study of the Hannahville Indian Community. East Lansing 1951.

Tucker, Glenn. Tecumseh: Vision of Glory. N.Y. Bobbs Merrill, 1956.

Wallace, Anthony F. C. The Death and Rebirth of the Seneca. N.Y. Knopf, 1970.

Winger, Otho. The Potowatomi Indians. Elgin Press, Elgin, Ill., 1839.

Tonquish. Mentioned in Michigan Pioneer and Historical Collections in the following: Volume 5, p. 398; Volume 8, p. 161–164; Volume 9, p. 7.

Tonquish mentioned in papers of Plymouth Historical Society members. File at the Burton Historical Society, Detroit.

Tonquish clan mentioned in the Julia Gatlin Moore Papers, Burton Historical Society.

Area Indians including Tonquish clan, or allied Indians mentioned in the following:

Christian, Dr. E. P. Historical Associations Connected with Wyandotte and Vicinity. MPHC. Vol. 13.

Coffinberry, S. C. Incidents connected with the First Settlement of Nottawa-Sippi Prairie in St. Joseph County. MPHC Vol. 2.

Clarkson, D. Pioneer Sketches. MPHC Vol. 1.

Indiana Historical Collections, 34 Vols. Indianapolis 1916–1951.

Utley, H. M. Plymouth. The First Settlement—Reminiscences of the Early History. MPHC Vol. 1.

Osband, Melvin D. My Recollections of Pioneers and Pioneer Life in Nankin. Vol. 24.

Chief Shavehead, et al. Volume 28. MPHC.

Kedzie, R. C. The St. Joes. MPHC Volume 28 (Including Shavehead, p. 161. 412–417)

Geddes, John. Ypsilanti Township, Its Settlement, etc. MPHC Vol. 4.

There are many other references to early Indians in MPHC. Consult Index.

Askin, John, The Askin Papers. 2 vols., M. M. Quaife, ed. Detroit, 1928.

Bald, F. Clever, Detroit's First American Decade. New York, 1938.

Brown, Henry D., et. al. Cadillac and the Founding of Detroit. Detroit, 1976.

Burton, Clarence M. The City of Detroit, 101–1922. Chicago, 1922.

Burton, Clarence M. Fort Ponchartrain du Detroit, 1701–1710, under Cadillac. Michigan Pioneer and History Collection, vol. 29.

Cadillac Papers. MPHC, vols., 33–34.

Cadillac's Village, a brochure published by the Detroit Historical Museum.

Canadian Archives Publications, 14 vols. Government Printing Bureau, Ottowa, 1902.

Canadian Historical Review. (Quarterly) U. of Toronto Press, See Index.

Catlin, George B. The Story of Detroit. Detroit News, 1923.

Charlevoix, Pierre Francois Xavier De, S.J. Histoire de la Nouvelle France. Paris, 1744. (Shea Translation) 6 vols., 1900.

Cooley, Thomas McIntyre, Michigan: a History of Governments. Boston, 1885.

Crowley, Mary Catherine, A Daughter of New France. Boston, 1901.

Cunningham, Wilbur M. Land of Four Flags. Grand Rapids, 1961.

Delanglez, Jean. Life and Voyages of Louis Joliet, 1645–1700. Chicago, 1948.

Dunbar, Willis Frederick. Michigan: A History of the Wolverine State. Grand Rapids, 1965.

Farmer, Silas. The History of Detroit. 2 Vols. Detroit, 1889.

Hennepin, Father Louis. A New Discovery of a Vast Country. Chicago, 1903.

Jones, Father Arthur, Old Huronia (5th Annual Report of Ontario Bureau of Archives) Toronto, 1908.

Kellogg, Louise Phelps, ed., Early Narratives of the Northwest. N.Y., 1917.

Kennedy, J. H. Jesuit and Savage in New France. New Haven, 1950.

Lahontan, Baron De, New Voyages to North America. 2 Vols., R. G. Thwaites ed. Chicago, 1905.

Laut, Agnes C. Cadillac. Indianapolis, 1931.

Margry, Pierre. Documents et etablissements des Francois. Paris, 1876.

Marquis, Thomas G. The Jesuit Missions (Chronicles of Canada series.) Toronto, 1916.

Michigan History Magazine (See index). Many articles about Early Detroit.

Nute, Grace L. The Voyageurs. N.Y. 1931.

Nute, Grace L. Caesars of the Wilderness. N.Y. 1943.

Ohio Historical Collections, 10 Vols. (Ohio State Archaeological & Historical Society). Columbus.

Ontario's Papers and Records. Ontario's Historical Society, Toronto.

Pare G. W. The Catholic Church in Detroit. 1701–1838. Detroit, 1951

Parkman, Francis, France and England in North America. Boston 1896.

Parkins, Almon E. Historical Geography of Detroit. 1918 Reissue (Kennikat Press, 1970).

Pierson, George W. Tocqueville and Beaumont in America. New York, 1938.

Pound, Arthur. Detroit, Dynamic City. Appleton, N.Y. 1940.

Quaife, M. M. Detroit Biographies. (Burton Historical Leaflets). Detroit 1930.

Wood, Edwin O. Historic Mackinaw. 2 Vols. N.Y. 1918.

Wrong, George M. The Conquest of New France. N.Y. 1928.

Luther Lincoln

Augustine, Robertson M. Indians, Sawmills, and Danes. Flat River Historical Society, 1921.

Chapman's History of Kent County.

Kent Country Records. Grand Rapids County Court.

Lincoln Documents. Michigan Room of the Grand Rapids Public Library.

Luther Lincoln

"Luther Lincoln, Pioneer Millwright," Grand Rapids Herald, Dec. 13, 1896.

Lincoln's History of Hingham, Mass. Burton Historical Library, Detroit.

Lincoln Family of Massachusetts. New England Historic & Genealogical Collection (See Index. Many References). Burton Library.

Montcalm County Records. Montcalm County Court House, Stanton, Mich.

Records of Oakfields Twp. Kent Co.

Records of Spencer Twp., Kent County.

Western Michigan Genealogical Society. Grand Rapids Library.

NOTES